PERGAMON INSTITUTE
(OXFORD)

Materials for Language Practice

WRITE RIGHT

WRITE RIGHT

A guide to effective communication in English

Taya Zinkin

PERGAMON PRESS

Oxford · New York · Toronto · Sydney · Paris · Frankfurt

UK	Pergamon Press Ltd, Headington Hill Hall, Oxford OX3 0BW, England
USA	Pergamon Press Inc, Maxwell House, Fairview Park, Elmsford, New York 10523, USA
CANADA	Pergamon of Canada, Suite 104, 150 Consumers Road, Willowdale, Ontario M2J 1P9, Canada
AUSTRALIA	Pergamon Press (Aust) Pty Ltd, PO Box 544, Potts Point, NSW 2011, Australia
FRANCE	Pergamon Press SARL, 24 rue des Ecoles, 75240 Paris, Cedex 05, France
FEDERAL REPUBLIC OF GERMANY	Pergamon Press GmbH, 6242 Kronberg-Taunus, Pferdstrasse 1, Federal Republic of Germany

First edition 1980

British Library Cataloguing in Publication Data

Zinkin, Taya
Write right.
1. English language — Text-books for foreigners
2. English language — Composition and exercises
I. Title II. Pergamon Institute of English
808'.042   PE1128   79-42941
ISBN 0-08-024566-8 Flexicover

Printed and bound in Great Britain by A. Wheaton & Co. Ltd., Exeter

TO SCARLETT EPSTEIN

with

FOND ADMIRATION

Contents

viii   **Contents**

Foreword

Taya Zinkin really needs no introduction from me, or indeed from anyone else. Over many years she built up an enviable reputation as the Indian Correspondent of *The (Manchester) Guardian* and *The Economist*. She is also the author of a number of books on India, has written for children and more recently has published a number of volumes of autobiography which were received with acclaim by the critics. Her writing is marked by its perceptiveness as well as its literary style, so she is eminently qualified to teach the craft of writing.

The idea of this book arose out of a project I was directing which involved the training of African and Asian students for Doctoral research in the Social Sciences. These students were all academically qualified and well read, but it was clear that they faced difficulties in expressing themselves adequately in English, particularly when it came to presenting a complex argument. Such students do not only need to speak and understand English; they must acquire the skill of writing letters, essays and theses in acceptable English, too. It was with this in mind that I invited Taya Zinkin to give several talks to a group of twelve of my Asian graduate students during the academic year 1977/ 78 when she was Research Associate at the University of Sussex. These talks were so well received and turned out to be so helpful that I suggested she ought to set out her ideas on the subject more systematically and for a wider audience. The result is the present book.

There is no doubt in my mind that large numbers of foreign students will regard this book as an indispensable tool when they embark upon secondary or tertiary education which demands full command of English. Even many students for whom English is the mother tongue might have much to learn from Taya Zinkin on how to *Write right*.

T. Scarlett Epstein
University of Sussex
August 1979

ix

Introduction

When writing anything, a letter, an essay, a memorandum, an application or an examination paper, the first thing you must decide is what it is you actually want to say.

This sounds terribly easy. Why write anything unless you have something to say? But, in fact, writing is not easy. Many people simply plunge into the middle of what they want to say and go on from there. They write as the ideas pour into their heads, without order or consistency.

To write clearly is very difficult. To convey your exact meaning you must first get a sense of the whole. This has to be done before you start to write. Next, the most important thing is to order your thoughts. After deciding what to say, you must decide in which order to say it. For this it is absolutely essential to sort out what is important and what is not. Only then should you start to write.

However, there are cases when it does not matter whether you have organized your thoughts or not: for example, when writing a personal letter to a friend, a relative or an intimate correspondent. For such letters it may indeed be better to let your pen follow the trend of your thoughts. Some of the best letters were written as if the author was talking to his reader.

But, of course, such a spontaneous and unstructured flow is out of the question when writing a business or a formal letter. On most occasions, excluding intimate correspondence, before putting pen or pencil to paper, a structure is required. And structure means an elaborate process of control. To achieve this control there are a number of rules which should make writing much easier. They should help to improve communication and the transfer of information, to pass examinations, to present essays or theses, to write reports or memoranda, to take the Minutes of a meeting, or to make a favourable impression when applying for a job.

In the first part of this book I have run quickly through a number of basic rules in order to refresh the reader's memory and to introduce him, perhaps, to one or two useful techniques for writing consecutive passages of English. In the second part I have examined a number of specific kinds of writing tasks in which those techniques might be applied. Each part is followed by materials for practice.

It is hoped that this will be a useful aid both for non-English speakers following study courses through the medium of English and for English-speaking school-leavers who are required to produce passages of written English as part of their daily life.

Taya Zinkin
London, 1979

PART ONE: SOME SIMPLE PRECEPTS

1. Decide what you want to say

A few lucky people are blessed with such orderly minds that they know instinctively not only what they want to say, but also how, and in what order, they want to say it. However, most people are not such clear thinkers. Even when they know what they want to say, they may have to decide how they want to say it. To be most effective they have to work things out first. Let us look at some examples of how this might be done.

Example 1. What makes a good friend?

Before starting to write an essay in answer to this question, jot down on a piece of paper the thoughts which come to mind. Write one thought per line. Suppose this is the result:

Reliability
Trustworthiness
Unselfishness
Availability
Community of interest
Complementarity of interests
Understanding
Relaxing
Shared sense of humour

Here are nine attributes of friendship. These are not the only ones. You may, of course, think of very different ones and of many more. However, to plan the shape of this essay let us assume that these nine are the ones you have chosen. First look at the list. Then decide on the order of importance and number each attribute accordingly. The arguments will then fall into a logical order. You are now ready to write. You can start with the least important and work up to the most important attribute. Or you can start the other way round and begin with the most important quality you look for in a friend. As long as the

3

order is logical it is entirely up to you which way you go.

If the proposition is more complicated than in this first example you will have to be particularly careful to work things out beforehand to avoid confusion, contradiction or both. Nothing is easier than to begin by saying one thing and then produce arguments to the contrary.

Example 2. TV: Does it weaken the family?

As in Example 1 jot down your thoughts, one per line. Give each line a letter of the alphabet. This helps to deal with increased complexity, as you will see. Suppose you jotted down the following thoughts:

A. Togetherness
B. TV dinners
C. Silence
D. Children unwanted
E. Common experiences

It is obvious from the list that TV weakens, as well as strengthens, the family. On the weakening side there are B, C and D. On the strengthening side there are A and E. The problem which has to be settled before starting to write is whether A + E are more important than B + C + D. In order to decide let us spell out what is meant by these five thoughts. First let us look at B + C + D.

B. TV Dinners

They replace family meals.

(a) this reduces the mother's role from being a much-loved cook to the hasty maker of sandwiches;
(b) the meal itself used to be a time for the generations to meet at leisure and exchange experiences. Now it is a silent affair.

C. Silence

Not only at meals, but whenever the TV is on. This greatly reduces communication between members of the family.

D. Children unwanted

(a) parents want to watch in peace;

(b) some programmes are unsuitable for children;
(c) children are sent out of the room;
(d) if there is no separate room for them they may even be sent outside.

Deal with B, C and D by scribbling next to each some key words from this analysis in order to help you remember. Now let us look at A and E.

A. Togetherness

(a) in Britain, before TV, the husband went out alone to the pub. Now he stays at home and the consumption of draught beer has fallen dramatically in favour of take-away beer, because husband and wife drink and watch together;
(b) children stay home to watch.

B. Common experience

(a) parents and children watch together;
(b) in the case of sports, this can bring the father much closer to his children because:
   (i)   they may be too small to be taken to the stadium or the cricket ground;
   (ii)   it may be too expensive to take them;
   (iii) or too complicated;
   (iv)   girls can watch football and boys show-jumping;
(c) TV provides common experience of world affairs, films, serials, etc.
(d) it even unites members of the family who are away and watch the same programmes: for example, parents and a married daughter;
(e) common experience has a cohesive effect.

Scribble against A and E key words to remember what is implied. After examining the pros and cons, decide whether TV strengthens or weakens the family.
I am inclined to argue that, on balance, it strengthens the family. But, of course, there is no right or wrong answer. The answer you should give is the answer you believe to be right. All that is required is that the case should be argued clearly, logically and convincingly. To do this it

W.R.—B

is important to re-order the original set of thoughts in the order in which you are going to use them. But do not ignore the arguments against the case you are making. Decide which are important enough to be mentioned, and in what order. Then decide where to put them. They can be disposed of at the beginning or after the case has been argued, or it may sometimes be better to put them in as you go along. For instance, TV brings the family together because children and parents watch the programmes but sometimes it separates them because parents want to watch in peace.

Having decided on the order, look at A and E again and think of examples. Number the examples before using them. Numbering helps to keep to a logical order.

It should now be easy to write a clear and logical discussion on the effects of TV on the family, or any subject of similar complexity.

Next, let us take a more complicated case. At first glance it may seem as simple as the previous example, but it is not.

Example 3. The car. Does it weaken the family?

Begin as with Example 1; jot down your thoughts, one per line. Then, as in Example 2, give a letter to each line. Below is a very incomplete list:

A. Easy Travel
B. Cheaper if many in family
C. Children love cars
D. Babies and paraphernalia
E. Flexibility
F. Wife also drives
G. Visits to relatives
H   Greater distances
I.   Shorter distances
J.   Mobility
K. Borrowing car

Here are eleven thoughts (you may, of course, have others). Some, like A, F, H, J and K can be used, as we shall see, to argue that cars strengthen *or* weaken the family. On the other hand B, C, D, E, G and

I can only be used in one way: they strengthen the family. The ambivalence of A, F, H, J and K means that instead of having eleven thoughts to organize there are sixteen.

A, F, H, J and K can be used to prove one thing or its opposite because:

A. Easy travel

This means that families can be scattered yet remain in close contact. However, it also means that families get more scattered. When people are far apart they tend to see less of each other than when they live within walking distance.

F. The wife also drives

Means that she can go out *without* her husband. On the other hand, they *share* an interest and she can drive him to work etc.

H, J. Greater and shorter distances

The mobility can weaken or strengthen the family; same argumens as for A.

K. Borrowing car

When older children borrow parental cars it can make for greater friendship. On the other hand, it also means that children get away more.

As can be seen from the above, the effect of the car on the family is more difficult to assess than the effect of TV. Therefore it becomes even more important to organize oneself before starting to write. The best way is to decide what one wants to say and then to put a ring around the letters which support the case. Let us assume you want to prove that the car weakens the family. Ring F, H, J and K. You may have decided that A and H are sufficiently alike not to bother about A. Having ringed the letters you are going to use, number them in order of importance. Now you are ready to write.

Proceed as with television, but in clearly ambivalent cases it is better to give the cons together with the pros.

2. Present it well

Having decided on what to say, say it neatly, clearly, simply, coherently and consistently. Presentation is very important. It makes reading faster and easier. It shows concern for the reader and it always pays to take the trouble.

1. Write neatly

Try to be legible. Corrections should be easy to follow. It is better to cross out than to alter. Insert the correction above the crossed out text if there is no room on the same line. When there is not enough room above the text, enter the correction in the margin and indicate its place with an arrow.

Neatness is particularly important when filling in forms or writing letters of application for jobs. It can be useful to fill the form in lightly with a soft pencil first and then to erase with a soft eraser after making the entries in ink. Obviously a neatly-filled application form or a neatly-written letter of application will make a better impression on a prospective employer than a messy one.

Neatness of presentation also matters a great deal in examinations. Neatness is not a substitute for knowledge, but a messy presentation can lower the marks which the answers receive. Many examiners down-grade for sloppiness.

2. Write clearly

Clarity is very important. Keep sentences short. Avoid complicated constructions with unnecessary subordinate clauses. Subordinate clauses can be clumsy and sometimes obscure. It is far better to cut long sentences into short ones by the use of punctuation.

Here is an example of how *not* to write. It is taken from a Government publication:

'In turn, India is exporting increased quantities of non-traditional goods like engineering products, machinery, components, equipment, electronic goods etc for which there is a growing demand among the non-aligned countries, and which India offers not only at a competitive price, but on comparatively easier financial terms and with facilities of after-sale service.'

It would be better to say:

'India is exporting increased quantities of non-traditional goods like engineering products, machinery, components, equipment, electronic goods etc. There is a growing demand for such goods among the non-aligned countries. India offers competitive prices, comparatively easier financial terms and facilities for after-sale service.'

One long sentence has been cut into three, and made simpler and clearer. Another clumsy sentence from the same source:

'While the increase in the prices of crude oil had benefited mainly the Arab countries, it made the non-aligned countries think hard on how best to meet their own requirements of trade and commerce by exchange of goods and services among themselves because of the paucity of hard currency reserves which were solely earmarked for the import of oil and oil products.'

There is nothing grammatically wrong with that sentence, but it is very heavy and long.

'The increase in the prices of crude oil has benefited mainly the Arab countries. This has made the non-aligned countries think hard how best to meet their requirements of exchange of goods and services among themselves. They have a paucity of hard currency reserves because these are earmarked for the import of oil and oil products.'

Notice what has been left out. However, it might be easier to re-write it altogether. In order to do this one has to work out what the author is trying to say. This is what he might have written had he tried to be clear:

'The rise in the price of crude oil has benefited mainly the Arab countries. The non-aligned countries have just enough reserves of hard currency to import the oil and the oil products they need. Therefore they have been forced to think of ways by which they can exchange goods and services to meet their requirements.'

3. Plan your paragraphs

Paragraphs are key aids to clarity.

(i) Paragraphs usually start about a half-inch further to the right. They break the text into units. This makes reading, and understanding, easier. Alternatively, leave a line between them.

(ii) There should be only one theme — or topic — per paragraph. Therefore paragraphs help the organization of one's thoughts.

(iii) Each paragraph has to contain a topic sentence, that is a sentence stating the theme of the paragraph. This sums up for the reader what the writer is trying to say.

(iv) Each paragraph should end on a transition which introduces the next paragraph. This helps the reader to follow the structure of the reasoning.

Paragraphs can be one sentence short or many sentences long. One sentence paragraphs are used to indicate:

(a) Emphasis: eg 'That first encounter was traumatic.'
and
(b) that the theme is completely dealt with by the topic sentence;
or
(c) when recording conversations, to indicate a change of speaker: eg 'I know everything,' I said, looking him in the eyes. 'It was not me!'

Paragraphs can have many sentences, so long as the unity of the theme is preserved. There should be only one theme per paragraph. If the paragraph is a long one it may be desirable to put the topic sentence at the beginning. However, there is no hard and fast rule. The topic sentence can go wherever it fits best.

Very long paragraphs defeat the purpose of breaking up the text. In such cases it is a good idea to divide the material into more than one paragraph. Then, since the theme flows on from one paragraph to the next, a transition is not necessary. All that is required are link words at the beginning. This is best done by starting the new paragraph with *In addition* . . . , *Moreover* . . . , *Another aspect* . . . etc.

To avoid monotony, try to construct paragraphs of varying length and whenever possible have a short one between two long ones. Here are a few illustrations taken from Example 2 of the previous section. Take *Togetherness*. It will make one paragraph because it is fairly obvious and straightforward. *Common experience*, on the other hand, is best dealt with in three. In the first include (a) and (b) as well as (bi), (bii), (biii), (biv), and (c). However, because (d) introduces another dimension into the argument, that of physical distance, it warrants a paragraph to itself. Moreover, this has the advantage of producing a short one after a fairly long one. The third paragraph, also short would consist of (e).

As already stated, paragraphs require a topic sentence. The three in *Common experience* could have topic sentences along the following lines:

Paragraph one: 'Now that they have TV, parents and children watch together, sharing experiences as never before.'
Paragraph two: 'The sharing of experience made possible by TV extends beyond the home. Thus a married daughter. . .'
Paragraph three: 'It is obvious that this sharing of experience has a cementing effect. It is not just that knowledge is shared. . .'

These are only suggestions. It can be argued that putting the topic sentence at the beginning helps the reader to read faster and to understand better. However, as long as each has a topic sentence and its theme applies to the whole paragraph, there can be no hard and fast rules about where to put it.

There must be a transition between paragraphs. The last sentence of one should ease the reader into the next. Thus paragraph one of the above example, on *Common experience*, should end with something like: ' . . .But that is not all.' Paragraph two could end with 'This common experience has many implications.'

3. Write simply

Simple writing is much easier to read and to understand.

1. Avoid long words

English is a language of short words. Fowler, one of the authorities on the use of good English, quotes a passage from Milton's *Paradise Lost* in which 52 out of 56 words have only one syllable: he also quotes a passage from Tennyson's *Idylls of the King* in which only twelve out of 101 words have more than one syllable.

Long words interrupt the flow of thought and the reader may not understand them. Here are a few examples of long words and of the short words which would be better: abbreviated/*short*, necessitate/*need*, prevaricate/*quibble*, dessicate/*dry-up*, circumscribe/*limit*, multi-faceted/*many-sided*, tendermindedness/*tenderness*.

However, in some cases the long word is better because it describes the meaning more accurately. If all you mean is 'calm' do not use 'imperturbable'; keep 'imperturbable' to describe someone who cannot be aroused or upset.

There are occasions when long words are called for, because they either add to the meaning or improve the rhythm of the sentence. For example: 'The moon-landing was a magnificently memorable achievement,' is stronger than: 'The moon-landing was a great feat to remember.' While there is a role and a place for long words there is no excuse for using the inverted and clumsy long words so dear to some American academics, like 'experimentalize' for *experiment*, 'signaturize' for sign, 'attitudinize' for *strike attitudes* or 'focalize' for focus.

2. Avoid unnecessary words

Unnecessary words are words which add nothing to the meaning of the sentence.

'To the latter end, the Technology Company Organization is a relatively small, fundamentally business-oriented group, maintaining a necessary minimum of technical and administrative staff.'

Let us analyze that sentence. *To the latter end* means nothing in the context. In *Technology Company Organization*, the word 'Organization' is superfluous. In *relatively small*, since we are not told relative to what, the use of a comparative for 'small' is meaningless. *Fundamentally business-oriented group* is not very clear, but it probably means 'a group with a business attitude.' *Maintaining* is an ugly long word; 'with' would be enough to convey the meaning. This is what is left after all the unnecessary words are left out:

'The Technology Company is a small business group with a minimum of technical and administrative staff.'

Sixteen words instead of 25, and much easier to understand.

There are many kinds of unnecessary words. We shall mention only a few.

(i) Pleonasms

(ie* repetitions) eg* future prospects, past antecedents, each and every, if and when, unless and until, save and except, hearth and home, more preferable, the reason is because.

'Many countries are enacting legislation and regulations which circumscribe and limit the scope. . .' There are no less than two repetitions in that sentence 'legislation and regulation', 'circumscribe and limit'.

(ii) Words which make no sense

eg* past prospects, future antecedents. 'Prospect' means expectations *to come*, ie* in the future. You cannot have a past expectation happen in the future. Antecedent means what came before, ie* in the past. One cannot have what came in the past in the future.

The asterisks, the * signs which followed ie and eg in the preceding paragraph, were meant to draw attention to the way in which ie and eg should be used. As you know, they are short for Latin words which mean respectively 'that is' and 'for instance' or 'such as'. So ie introduces a definition; eg introduces an illustration. Avoid the common error of using one for the other.

(iii) Piling it on

'North India has been ravaged, maimed and wounded. . .' This is piling it on, and as a progression the order in which the words have been placed cancels their impact; 'wounded, maimed and ravaged' would have been more effective, since 'maimed' implies the loss of at least one limb and 'ravaged' implies total destruction. To end the progression with wounded is an anti-climax. In this case it would have been enough to say 'North India has been ravaged.'

Progressions can be effective if they are right, like this one from a novel by Surtees:
'Dinner lost! hounds lost, self lost — all lost together!'
One qualifying word per noun is a sound rule unless the qualifying words refer to quite different qualities. For instance, (eg), 'He is tall, dark and handsome.' He could be short, dark and ugly, or tall, blond and handsome.

3. Avoid long sentences

Short sentences make for clarity. Here is an example of what can happen when sentences get out of hand. Some of the unnecessary words have been put in brackets.

'This (presentation) is a 'case history', (not a single, in-depth technology transfer project, but rather) of a United States (basic) steel (technology source) enterprise — (in terms of) its approach to international transfer of its technologies, (its) objectives and (its) most compelling current problems, especially as regards (its present) dealings with and (future) prospects for technology transfer to the developing countries.'

Not a single full stop! That sentence is abominable. Even after leaving out most of the words which add nothing to the meaning, and the repetitions — such as 'future prospects' — it remains a heavy sentence and, more important, it is obscure. What is its author trying to say? Perhaps he meant something like:

'This is a study of the attitudes, objectives and major problems of an American steel company transferring technology internationally, especially to developing countries. It is not a full case-history of any one project.'

There are only 34 words instead of 61, and these have been split into two sentences. This was easy to do, because the part about its not being a full case-study is separate.

However, those 34 words still make a clumsy text which does not fully bring out the author's point. To get his full meaning, the sentence has to be re-written altogether:

'The transfer of technology to developing countries should be considered from three angles; the attitudes of the parties, their objectives, and th∠ difficulties which arise. This paper presents the point of view of one American steel company. However, no single project is studied in depth.'

45 words against the 34 of the revised original, but this way the first sentence states the general issue; the second sentence makes it clear that an illustration of this general issue has been given. That lays out the argument in its logical order. The addition of 'should be considered from three angles. . .' puts the problem of transferring technology into focus and provides three headings for later expansion. In the original sentence the logic was confused.

Here is another unnecessarily long sentence. It should not, with the previous example in mind, be difficult to decide which are the unnecessary words:

'It should be noted that, in the circumstances, until such time as investigations have been carried out with a view to ascertaining the facts of the matter in their own right, the Minister will not be in a position to make a precipitate judgment with regard to the appropriate procedure to maximize provisions for the fostering of the expansion of tourism to this country.'

In case a few of them were missed they have been put in brackets:

'(It should be noted that, in the circumstances) until (such time as) investigations have been carried out (with a view to ascertaining the facts of the matter of their own right,) the Minister will not be in a position to make a (precipitate) judgment (with regard to) [*add:* on] the (appropriate) procedure to maximize provisions for (the fostering of) the expansion of tourism to this country.'

Of those 64 words only 27 are relevant. Small wonder that the meaning gets lost. Did you guess what was meant? If not, here it is in plain English:

'The Minister cannot decide what to do to assist tourism until he has the facts.'

4. Avoid unnecessary sentences

An unnecessary sentence is one which:

— adds nothing to the meaning;
— repeats what has already been said; or
— creates a digression by introducing an irrelevance.

Here is an example of a sentence which repeats what has already been said:

'If experience is a good teacher, it is fair to say that most difficulties encountered in basically sound technology transfer arrangements result from a failure by one or both parties to treat the transfer as a partnership; and most of the problems treated in this discussion can, in most instances, be attributed to attempts by the involved government so to accommodate other, more general objectives as to lose the essential partnership elements of particular proposed transfers. In all the cases in which we have been involved, our problems have come from somebody not realising that transfer of technology requires a partnership.'

The second sentence essentially repeats the first. One or the other should be left out, preferably the first, since it is longer and less precise.

Here is another example of needless repetition:

'The control of women lies in the need to control their capacity for biological reproduction and female fertility.'

The only exceptions when repetitions are in order are:

(a) for emphasis:
    'Mozart died young; when he died he was not old even by the standards of those days. Indeed he was very young when he died.'
(b) after the arguments have been discussed, to show that the conclusion has been reached:

    'Therefore, as we have tried to show, TV unites the family.'

Example of a sentence which introduces a digression, ie an irrelevance:

'One of Mary's best friends is called Jane. Jane's uncle was in India during the war. Without Jane's help Mary could not have made the dress she wore for the dance.' Jane's uncle and his presence in India during the war have nothing to do with the rest of the text.

5. Avoid jargon

What is jargon? Roget's *Thesaurus* lists, under jargon, technical language, absurdity, meaninglessness, slang. According to Fowler, jargon is 'talk that is considered both ugly-sounding and hard to understand, applied especially to:

(i)   the sectional vocabulary of a science, art, class, trade, profession, full of technical terms;
(ii) mixed speech of different languages;
(iii) the use of long words, circumlocution and other clumsiness.'

Jargon is often used to cloak ignorance rather than act as an explanation of the issues.

(i) Technical terms out of context

'It may be more economically viable to substitute margarine for butter' (cheaper).

Sociologists are frequently guilty of jargon; eg they often call cousins 'members of the same kinship group'.

But the prize, perhaps, is won by Dr Kohn's quotation in the *New Scientist:*

> '. . .a set of arrangements for producing and rearing children the viability of which is not predicated on the consistent presence in the household of any adult male acting in the role of husband and father. . .'

which means:

'A way of having and bringing up children which does not depend on having a man there the whole time to act as husband and father.'

(ii) Mixed speech of different languages

This mixture often looks affected:
'I gave him *carte blanche*' (a free hand); 'what I always say in such cases is *cherchez la femme*' (look for the woman); 'by a simple substitution for 'Jew' Shylock's speech could read as the Afro-Asian's *cri de coeur*' (heart-felt call); 'let me tell you, just *entre nous*, I don't trust that man' (between ourselves).

(iii) Long words, circumlocutions, clumsiness

Here are a few examples:

"Jargon has visual unattractiveness" (is ugly); 'making precipitate judgments on the basis of temporary impressions' (jumping to conclusions).

A metaphor which is not vivid is jargon. (According to the *Concise Oxford Dictionary* a metaphor is the application of a name or a descriptive term to an object to which it is not strictly applicable.) Examples of bad metaphors (ie not vivid and therefore jargon):

'These houses should be broken down into types' (classified by types). 'The ceiling for the flooring of those houses. . .' (the limit in square feet, or perhaps in cost).

Sir Ernest Gowers quotes the following string of jargon gems:

> 'Manpower ceilings are a very blunt macro-instrument and will be either ineffective or unduly restrictive if not based on the results of management reviews and other 'micro' activities . . . ceilings are biting, but this is what they were meant to do.'

Sir Ernest's comment is apt:

> Unless you are accustomed to thinking of a ceiling as a blunt instrument that bites, you will be surprised.'

'Macro-instrument' and 'micro' activities are jargon too.

However, 'the jaws of a bulldozer biting into the hillside' is not jargon because it is an apt metaphor which adds vividness to the action of the bulldozer. Good metaphors are very effective in bringing home the point. Think of expressions like 'Iron Curtain', 'paper tiger', 'Domino theory', 'red herring', 'white elephant', 'wind of change', etc.

6. Avoid double negatives

They seldom mean what you think.
(1) A double negative does not equal a simple positive: eg 'Not uninteresting' does not mean 'interesting', it means 'mildly interesting', just as 'not without merit' means 'not totally devoid of merit', and not 'with merit'.
(2) Double negatives can be confusing because they make you stop to work out what is meant. 'There is no reason to believe that his argument is not true.' Following the self-cancellation of the double negative, this means that his argument is true. It is much better to say so.

7. Avoid mixing metaphors

A mixed metaphor is a sentence in which two metaphors are coupled, usually in an incongruous way, eg 'I smell a rat and will nip it in the bud'. 'I smell a rat' is a metaphor. You are applying the idea of smelling a rat in the literal sense to something being wrong in a general way. Equally, 'nip in the bud' is a metaphor. You apply the idea of frost killing the buds to stopping something at the very beginning. The idea of 'nipping a rat in the bud', however funny, is meaningless. As the rat is a fully grown animal, there is no beginning to be destroyed.

'The sacred cows which have come home to roost' are merely ridiculous, but no more so than the scientist's discovery of 'a virgin field pregnant with possibilities.' The virgin forest 'Where the hand of man has not yet set foot' may be incongruous, but it is clear; not so the wife's boast that her husband 'never crossed bridges with everybody'. Did she mean he never crossed his bridges before he had to? Or that he was prepared to cross swords with everybody? Better still, that he never burns his bridges before crossing them?

Here is an example of how not to write:

'The fabric of British society is being uprooted by change. Those centuries of effort which went into erecting the stratification of Britain's social and economic fabric is being felled at one fell swoop by the axe of taxation, inflation and wage restraint, axe which sweeps away differentials while flushing incentives and productivity down the drain in its wake. Unless the seeds of our social fabric can be nursed back to life and made to bloom once more, Britain, the mother of industrialization runs the grave risk of becoming a backward country.'

This is very badly written. It is too repetitive. The word fabric is used three times. There are two errors of grammar. It is not the fabric which is being felled but those centuries of effort, so that it should read 'are being felled. . .' and 'the axe of taxation, inflation and wage restraint' should either be 'the axes' or 'the combined axe'. Above all there are far too many mixed metaphors and some of the images are obscure. One can fell or uproot a tree, not centuries, nor a fabric. One can nurse seeds into bloom but not fabrics; stratifications cannot be erected and fabrics are not stratified. Axes are not instruments for sweeping or flushing and, unlike ships, they have no wake.

Here, by contrast, is an extract from a book review which appeared in *The Economist* (3 Feb 1979).

'There have been so many predictions of take-off into positive science which have turned out to be blind alleys that a feeling close to desperation overtakes the reader. Two hundred years of theorizing and empirical studies have certainly led to an appreciation and clarification of the possibilities of economic behaviour. We know more in the sense of being able, on the basis of abstract analysis and empirical investigation, to reject almost any simple proposition. But we know very little in the sense of being able to point to established laws or even tendencies, except for the most trivial. Above all the bright promise of the mathematical, econometric and computational revolution lacks fulfilment. The journals today are so high-powered that to a majority even of professional academics they are incomprehensible; but these mountains of technical skill produce only mice of results.'

Both mountains giving birth to mice and something turning into a blind alley are clichés, but they are not out of place in the context because they are meant to emphasize the criticisms of the book under review. Indeed positive science turning into a blind alley, like a mountain of technical skill giving birth to a mouse, are mixed metaphors with a pleasingly ironic sting in the tail. Equally 'econometric' and 'computational' are technical terms but their use is fully justified since they are economic terms in an article dealing with economics.

4. Be coherent and consistent

To be coherent is to make sense, to be easy to follow and easy to understand. To be coherent:

1. *Put the words of each sentence in the right place.*
2. *Put the sentences in the right order.*
3. *Avoid ambiguity.*

1. The basic unit for the written expression of thought is the sentence. To be complete the sentence must have at least one verb and one subject; the subject, however can be implied.

   If asked to make a sentence from the following jumbled words: the, the, ate, tiger, man, you would have no problem. The sentence can only be 'the tiger ate the man.' But, if, instead of tiger, there was the word pig, the sentence could be either 'the man ate the pig', or 'the pig ate the man'. Therefore, even in a very simple sentence it is the order of words which determines the meaning.

   Naturally, as the sentences become more complicated, the order of words becomes more important. For example: 'I am wearing the dress my mother made for my birthday' does not mean the same thing as 'I am wearing for my birthday the dress my mother made.' The difference in meaning comes from the place of 'for my birthday.' Keep together the words which belong together; failure to do so may yield some very odd results:

   'He took out his gun, blew his nose, wiped it clean, put it in his pocket and wondered whether it would go off.'

   The sentence was not meant to be funny; its author simply forgot to keep together the words which belonged together. It was the gun that he wiped clean, not his nose; the sentence ought to run like this: 'He blew his nose: took out his gun, wiped it clean, put it in his pocket and wondered whether if would go off.'

2. With sentences, as with words, it is very important to keep to the logical order. It is equally important to use short, simple sentences with one thought per sentence. Here are three good sentences:

> 'She rose, all woman, and all the best of woman, tender, pitiful, hating the wrong, loyal to her own sex. . . She tore off her nightcap and her hair fell about her in profusion. Undying coquetry awoke.' (R. L. Stevenson).

Each sentence contains one thought. The first sentence concerns itself with the qualities of the heroine; the second describes one action and its consequence; the third is about the heroine's feelings. Note how short the third sentence is: three words only. So few words make the sentence striking and therefore reinforce its meaning.

3. Avoid ambiguity. Ambiguity is not lack of coherence, but obscurity. Faulty construction can lead to misunderstanding or to nonsense. 'I shall eat at my home which is in London on Sunday.' As if home was not in London during the week. Had the words which belonged together been kept together there would have been no ambiguity. 'On Sunday I shall eat at my home which is in London' or 'I shall eat on Sunday at my home which is in London.'

Nothing is more irritating than to find the same word spelt in different ways. If one spells 'Muslim' with a 'u' and an 'i', one must not switch to 'Moslem' with an 'o' and an 'e'. The same applies to Mahomed/Mahomet, Koran/Quran, pandit/pundit, Czar/Tsar, yaourt/yoghurt, and to English words like cheque/check, through/thru, trans-ship/tranship, rhyme/rime.

5. Watch your punctuation

Punctuation is very important. Without it, words would follow each other in an endless stream and the meaning would be lost. The role of punctuation is to make the meaning clear. Here are a few simple rules of punctuation which are too often overlooked.

1. Full-stop

(a) Long-hand can be deceptive and full-stops can sometimes look like commas. It is therefore useful to remember to start the next word after a full-stop with a capital. That full-stops are necessary is shown by this school-boy favourite: 'King Charles spoke and walked an hour after his head was cut off.' There should be a full-stop after 'walked.'

(b) Three full-stops placed one after the other mean that words have been left out in a quotation; 'Let me tell you . . . I hope you agree.' or to indicate that the sentence has been left unfinished deliberately, 'I could go on and on. . .'

2. Colon

(a) The colon is used to introduce the words which follow it. 'My shopping list reads: 12 eggs, 1 lb butter, 2 lbs sugar. . .'

(b) To introduce direct speech or a quotation. Then he said: 'After all. . .'

3. Semi-colon

The semi-colon is very useful. It is less final than a full-stop. It can be used between sentences which are complete in themselves, to indicate that there is a connection between their meaning. 'I disliked her at first sight; she looked sloppy in her jeans and her kinky hair dyed green was unkempt.' A full-stop after 'sight' would cut off the trend of thought while the insertion of 'because' would weaken the meaning. Because the semi-colon is less than a full-stop but more than a comma it is useful to break up long sentences which already have commas in them. Here is an example taken from Samuel Johnson:

> 'The notice which you have been pleased to take of my labours, had it been early had been kind; but it has been delayed until I am indifferent, and cannot impart it; till I am known and do not want it.'

If Samuel Johnson had used full-stops instead of semi-colons he would have destroyed the dignity of this passage by making it jerky. Instead, by using semi-colons he adds weight to each of his reasons.

4. Comma

The comma is a useful stop, especially when reading out loud; it gives you time to breathe. There are as many different ways of using commas as there are styles of writing. However, here are nine different cases when commas must be used.

(a) Before and after speech: [but see also *colon* above]

'I must ask you to repeat these words,' said the priest, 'before I can pronounce you man and wife.'

(b) When listing things, qualities, ideas or clauses: 'Fear, love, hate, hunger and death are man's lot.' 'His dedication to office, his endless energy, his honesty and his generosity will long be remembered.'

(c) To separate words of the same part of speech:

'He advanced slowly, steadily, silently.' (adverbs)
'He is tall, dark, fat yet handsome.' (adjectives)
'He lied, stole, killed and fled.' (verbs)
'in walked the sailor, the soldier, the pilot. . .' (nouns).

(d) To separate from the rest of the sentence qualifying words and words not essential to its meaning: 'Napoleon, the French Emperor, was defeated at Waterloo.'

(e) To separate from the rest of the sentence a non-defining clause:

'The battle of Waterloo, which you will have read about, is one of the most important in history.'

(f) Between words repeated for emphasis:

'It was much, much too hot.'

(g) Instead of *or* and *and:*

'Give me apples, pears and prunes.' (I want all three).
'Give me apples, pears or prunes.' (I want only one of them.)

(h) Usually after and around *however*.

'However, you must forgive him.'
'Let us look at the facts, however, lest we do him an injustice.'

(i) Before *and* or *but* for special emphasis:

'I love him, but I do not want him to know this.'
'The house was thatched and whitewashed, and English was written on it, and on every foot of ground around it.'

'What the less developed countries need is more aid, a remission of debt, and above all, trade.' (*But* could be substituted for *and*.)

5. Question mark

There is only one use for the question mark: after a direct question.

(a) In speech:
'Do you want this?'

(b) In the text:
'Is he rich? I wonder.'

Note that 'I wonder if he is rich' takes no question mark: it is not a question.

6. Exclamation mark

Use it very seldom. A good rule is to keep exclamation marks almost exclusively for exclamations. 'Oh!', 'What a shame!', 'What a stupid thing to say!' shouted the man. 'You fool!' used as abuse, not as a statement of IQ. Too many exclamation marks suggest inability to express oneself. Exclamation marks should be used sparingly.

7. Inverted commas

These can be used:

(a) to single out words or letters.

(b) to indicate that the words between them are a quotation:

It was reported in the press that: 'In 1973, more than 43 million prescriptions for sedatives. . . '

(c) to indicate that the words between them are part of direct speech: 'We are a group of serious people. . .'

(d) to indicate that the words between them are the title of a book or a newspaper:

It was reported in 'The Times' that millions of prescriptions. . . or, to keep to the sentence quoted:

This is what was reported in "The Times": 'In 1973, more than 43 million prescriptions. . .' However, to have inverted commas with a different use, so close to each other, looks clumsy. Therefore, it is better to put "The Times" in italics, or when italics are not available, to use single inverted commas, thus: This is what was reported in 'The Times': "In 1973. . ."

(e) Inverted commas can be single or double. Another occasion when it is necessary to use both kinds is when there is a quotation within a quotation. Here is an example:

The following report appeared in 'The Guardian': "A doctor once described his method of finding out what was wrong with his patients. 'Well,' he would start, 'What is wrong?' Never accepting the first answer, he would continue: 'And what else?' And again: 'What else' and again and again." Note the use of single inverted commas for the name of the newspaper and for the direct speech quoted in the article. This is in contrast with the double inverted commas which mark the beginning and the end of the quoted passage.

Finally, there are occasions on which two types of inverted commas are not enough as in the following passage from Dickens' *David Copperfield:*

> Then, turning affectionately to me, with her cheeks against mine, "Am I a naughty mama to you, Davy? am I a hasty, cruel, selfish, bad mama? Say I am, my child; say 'yes', dear boy, and Pegotty will love you; and Pegotty's love is a great deal better than mine, Davy. I don't love you at all, do I?"

"Yes" has to be in different kind of inverted commas from the main speech to indicate that it is the child who is asked to say it. Since there are only two kinds of inverted commas the entire passage has been indented, that is set out in a way which shows that it is not part of the main text.

8. Brackets

These are used:

(a) to introduce words which do not affect the meaning of the text or affect it only in a subordinate way:
'I have already dealt with the use of inverted commas within a quotation (see above). Punctuation (including the use of brackets) makes for easier reading.'
In the above example the brackets can be replaced by commas.

(b) to set out numbers or letters of the alphabet used to enumerate lists; eg (i), (ii), (iii); (a), (b), (c),. . .

(c) square brackets [ ] are best used to enclose words which have nothing to do with the meaning of the text. Instructions for the printers for instance or a little note to oneself to remind one of something: [insert an example to illustrate the use of square brackets.]

9. Hyphen

Use hyphens:

(a) to make compound words: 'vice-president', 'public-house', 'son-in-law', 'know-how'.

(b) to unite two or more words in order to make them into an adjective. 'War-time, 'never-to-be-forgotten event', 'well-to-do', 'good-for-nothing', 'first-class'.

(c) after certain Latin prefixes: 'anti-English', 'post-independence', 'ex-Prime Minister', 'pre-independence'.

10. Dash

Use the dash:

(a) to summarize a list already given: 'Beauty, determination, talent — this is what makes a star.'

(b) to emphasize the end of a sentence: 'The battle of Waterloo — Victor Hugo wrote a poem about it — was lost by France.'

To end this chapter here is a classic example to show how important punctuation can be:

'The teacher', said the student, 'is an ass,'
does not mean the same thing as:
The teacher said: 'the student is an ass.'

6. Practice

Essays

Discuss the following:

1. Should parents pay their children for doing chores? (baby-sitting, shoe-shining, washing-up, washing the car etc.)
2. The pros and cons of working one's way through college.
3. The effect of legal polygamy on the status of women.
4. Does contraception undermine morality?
5. Does the lowering of coming of age weaken the family?
6. Does showing violence on TV increase crime?

Punctuation

Punctuate the following paragraphs:

1. The British health service is no longer even if it ever was the envy of the world nor however is it on the point of collapse with such measured conclusions has the Royal Commission on the health service handed down the sort of urbane judgments one has come to expect from such bodies but on one point the commission's findings came through loud and clear that the 1974 reorganization of Britains greatest post-war social institution has in practice been a disaster doctors nurses patients even the administration themselves have come to spend an exhausting expensive and demoralizing amount of their time wrestling with a bureaucratic octopus (*The Economist* 21 July 1979, p 16)

2. Those to whom God has given the gift of comely speech should not hide their light beneath a bushel but should willingly show it abroad if a great truth is proclaimed in the ears of men it brings forth fruit a hundred fold but when the sweetness of the telling is praised of many flowers mingle with the fruit upon the branch (*French Mediaeval Romances* translated by E. Mason, Everyman's Library Edition 1924, p. 1.

3. Now on a day the Queen had fallen asleep after meat and on her awaking would walk a little in the garden she called her companion to

her and the two went forth to be glad amongst the flowers as they looked across the sea they marked a ship drawing near the land rising and falling upon the waves very fearful was the Queen thereat for the vessel came to anchorage though there was no helmsman to direct her course the dames face became sanguine for dread and she turned about to flee her maiden who was of more courage than she stayed her mistress with many comforting words for her part she was very desirous to know what this thing meant she hastened to the shore and laying aside her mantle climbed within this wondrous vessel thereon she found no living soul save only the knight sleeping fast within the pavilion the damsel looked long upon the knight for pale he was as wax and well she deemed him dead she returned forthwith to the Queen and told her of this marvel and of the good knight who was slain let us go together on the ship replied the lady if he be dead we may give him fitting burial and the priest shall pray for his soul should he be yet alive perchance he will speak and tell us of his case (As(2) p 9).

4. In their sun-splashed islands West Indians are generally gay friendly talkative people accustomed to greeting each other whether stranger or friend with a wave a nod a wink or hi man they see each other look each other in the face in hope of recognizing someone from the same town village street school or place of employment and if on another island they look into each others faces in the hope of recognizing someone from home (*Paid Servant* by E. R. Braithwaite, Bodley Head 1962, p. 73).

Rearrangement and paragraphing.

Put order into the following texts by breaking them into short paragraphs, making sure they are linked together and removing unnecessary words or sentences:

1. Yesterday I had an exhausting day. At five o'clock I rushed out for a last minute shopping spree. I woke up at dawn because of a misguided telephone call. It was a wrong number. Lunch was late because I had to do the ironing first. I hurriedly swallowed my breakfast as there were so many things I had to get done. I had been delayed in getting up because the hot water was cold so that I had to boil two kettles of water to take the chill off my bath. I had no option but to wind an exotic scarf around my head to hide my hair, it matched my party dress, fortunately. After lunch I cleaned

the flat so that it would look nice for my guests. It was not possible to wash my hair. No hot water, remember! At last the table was laid, the dinner ready, the room cosy, I did not have time to go to the hairdresser, what a mess! Thank God my scarf matched my dress. The bell rang, it was my first guest.

2. Asian girls are taught to be patient and to give up things for their brothers whether older or younger. Sometimes elder brothers are taught to give their best things to their young sisters. A son always gets the bigger and better helping of food. Girls must not quarrel with elder brothers. Elder sisters must be patient and make sacrifices. Sisters generally do not mind. Boys get preference in everything. From early childhood girls know that boys are entitled to the biggest share.

3. In many developing countries when they are very small both boys and girls wear short pants. From early childhood children wear different clothes on the basis of sex. Girls of about seven or eight wear a skirt and a blouse or a frock. Boys stay in pants or wear a kind of loin cloth, and sometimes a shirt. Boys and girls usually go barefoot until they get into their teens. In Muslim countries girls must be covered from the time of puberty. Some girls have to wear a veil, others a tent-like cover with holes for the eyes, others must cover their head with a shawl or a corner of their sari. It all depends on how religious and conservative their society is. Many aborigines in Asia and Africa go about without covering their breasts. Those girls who do not belong to orthodox Islamic cultures do not have to cover themselves. Masai girls and women do not cover their breasts.

4. About half the world's population are women, yet little is done to do research on them. I have consulted, perused and read all the published and unpublished material on women and have also made my own observations. Some books have recently been published on women. Some reports have also been recently published on the same subject. Overpopulation is one of the greatest problems in the world. As there is a great gap in the literature on the understanding of women and society I propose to try to find out

how women see themselves and how they see their problems. I
have analyzed men's position and compared it with women's
position in order to avoid painting a biased picture of women's
position. When studying women's position it is necessary to
examine their life cycle. The status of women changes with their
life cycle. There is a lot of difference in the status of a married
woman and that of a young girl or that of a widow.

Rewriting

Rewrite the following passages, which are examples of how not to write:

A. simplify;
B. identify the unnecessary words, stating your reasons; and
C. split the paragraphs into shorter ones making sure they are properly
   linked.

1. These experiences, exemplifying expressed concerns about the
   future course of technology transfer for development and, rela-
   tedly, the course of international commercial relations in a context
   of fair trade for the mutual benefit of the trading partners con-
   cerned, are illustrated by several examples of actual technology
   transfers, of varying degrees of 'success' as assessed from the
   viewpoint of the proprietor of those technologies.

2. The present and future course of the foreign commerce of the
   United States is so heavily dependent upon a resolution, satisfac-
   tory both to this country and to foreign trade partners, of the
   existing and impending problems related to these factors, that a
   prompt, intensive governmental review and policy development
   program, well coordinated with the private sectors, is amply justified.

3. The technologies comprising or based upon the products and
   services outlined above under industry and technology characteri-
   zation and which constitute the Company's lines of business and
   expertise, normally are made available to any interested party to
   whom the technology can be transferred consistent with applicable laws and obligations to others, provided that the proposed

recipient is financially responsible and the available terms, importantly including payment for and protection of involved industrial property rights, are considered reasonable. The Company maintains active and extensive research and development organizations and efforts in support of most of these business activities. New technical developments arising from these efforts also are covered by such technology transfer policy.

4. Resource development. Due in largest measure to absence of experience or prospective depletion of the United States natural resources, the Company long has been active in worldwide exploration for and development of the raw materials needed for domestic production of the products of the steel and related industries — primarily metalliferous ores, such as those of iron, manganese, chromium, zinc, nickel, copper, as well as more 'exotic' metals such as titanium, platinum. To that extent, the Company fits an international economic system pattern complained of by some of the developing countries. However, increasingly such foreign operations are carried out by joint ventures, often of minority Company interest, with foreign private enterprise or governments. As in the case of the foreign manufacturing ventures, and with some important exceptions, technology transfer to such resource development ventures often is more characterizable as an 'incident' to the enablement of such enterprises to carry out the intended commercial development objectives rather than the prime objective of the arrangement. Company technologies as may be required for construction and operation of mines and/or benefication or other upgrading of semi-finishing facilities, in many cases are not broadly patentably unique — but are of considerable commercial significance in aggregate advantage to the technical proficiencies and economies of such operations.

PART TWO: SOME SPECIAL TASKS

7. Writing a letter

A letter is a substitute for direct contact. One writes to people instead of being with them or talking to them on the telephone. It is also a way of making sure that there is a record of things which require proof. This is why a business telephone call is often followed by a letter of confirmation. For example, if you lose your credit card you ring up the relevant department at once to inform it and follow this up in writing.

Whatever the reason for writing, letters represent their author. This is one of the reasons people are often required to apply for a job in writing. To make a good impression, it is worth taking trouble.

There are at least five types of letter:

— intimate letters;
— formal private letters;
— business letters;
— official letters;
— letters of application.

Hand-written letters should be legible; typed ones should be neat. Whether hand-written or typed, letters should be carefully set out with margins on both sides.

The recipient of any letter needs to know who the sender is. Signatures can be illegible and may never have been seen before. Imagine getting a letter of invitation for dinner for Saturday week signed illegibly or signed simply 'John'. Therefore it is usual to put the sender's address in the top right-hand corner. This helps to identify him. It also means that one does not have to hunt for the address when answering.

Always put the date. The best place is in the top right corner below the sender's address. People sometimes write the date like this: '11.3.78'. But this can lead to confusion, because some people put the day before the month while others put the month first. Confusion does not arise at the time; you know whether you are in March or November, but it may arise later and cause problems. This is why it is better to write the date 'March 11, 79' or '11th March 1979'.

If the letter is going to be short, try to set it out so that it fills the page. Start low, with wide margins. If the letter is long do not forget to number the pages.

How to begin varies with the kind of letter. 'Dear John,' or 'Dear Mr Smith,' if it is an acquaintance, depending on how well you know him. 'Dear Sir,' or 'Dear Sirs,' if the address is a firm. 'Dear Mrs Smith,' or 'Dear Miss Smith,' or 'Dear Ms Smith,' if the addressee is a woman, but *never* 'Dear Miss,' or 'Dear Madam'. And never write 'Dear Mr John Smith,' or 'Dear Mrs Jane Smith'. Either the surname, or the Christian name: never both.

Always put a comma after 'Dear. . . ,' 'Dear Mr Smith,' 'Dear John,' or 'Dear Mrs Smith,' etc. End usually with 'Yours sincerely', but when you start with 'Dear Sir,' end with 'Yours faithfully'. Never put a comma or a full-stop after 'sincerely' or 'faithfully'; put nothing.

Unless the addressee is a friend, put his name and address on the left of the page, just below the level of the date (which is on the right). This saves time if further correspondence is needed and will act as proof, if required, that the letter was written.

Keep a copy of the letter. If your signature — which comes under 'Yours sincerely' or 'Yours faithfully' — is not legible, print your name underneath in brackets. If you are a woman add 'Mrs', 'Miss' or 'Ms'.

Here are some examples of how to write letters. Before starting to compose decide what it is you want to say. Then say it simply, clearly and with paragraphs.

1. Answering a letter

What does the writer want?

Make sure you answer his questions or points.

Suppose you receive a reminder from a shop asking you to pay for its goods and that your cheque is already in the post. Your letter should be something like this:

| *Mr XYZ* | Ref: your invoice No. | *your address* |
| *address* | | *date* |

Dear Sir,

Thank you for your letter of . . . . .*(date)*
I have already mailed you £. . . . by cheque No. . . . .
dated . . . .

Yours faithfully

Signature

Note that the letter contains all the information required by both sender and recipient. His references are the invoice number and the date of his letter. Your reference is the number of the cheque (in case it should get lost in the post and you have to stop it and issue another one.)

If you know the shopkeeper personally you might call him 'Dear Mr XYZ,' and add a sentence to say you are sorry he is put to inconvenience by postal delays, and sign 'Yours sincerely'.

2. Writing a letter of complaint

Here you are not answering somebody else's point but making a point which somebody else has to answer. Make the point simply and clearly and give all the relevant details in their relevant order.

Suppose you are writing to complain about a defective purchase. Your letter should be something like this:

| *The Manager* | *address* |
| *The Electrical. . .* | *date* |

Dear Sir,

On .*date*. I purchased from your shop a vacuum cleaner (*give name of the make, the name of the Model, the serial number if you can read it*) for £. . . .

It does not work. Could you please arrange to have it put in order?

Yours faithfully

Signed

Perhaps no action has been taken and you have to write again. You should document your case as much as you can. If you have a spare copy (or can make one) of the first letter, enclose it. Make sure you have an extra copy in case of need. And if you threaten the shop with further action it is only fair to let them know what you propose to do. Indeed, this usually acts as a spur.

Your letter should now run something like this:

The Manager   *address*
The Electrical. . .   *date*

Dear Sir,

Would you please refer to my letter (*or letters*) of . . . . (*date or dates*) copy (*or copies*) of which is/*are* attached.

I have received no answer so far.

Do you want me to report the matter to the Consumer Council?

I would be grateful for an answer within a week.

Yours faithfully
Signed
. . . Enclosures (*give the number*)

By enclosing the copy of previous correspondence you make it impossible for the Manager to plead ignorance. Even if he did not receive your letter dated. . . , he now has before his eyes a copy of it. By writing 'Enclosures,' and giving their number (you may have written many times) you make it impossible for someone in the office to throw away the carbons. If they get separated from the letter by mistake, they will be looked for.

3. Writing an official letter (ie a letter sent to a public authority)

The principles are the same as far as for other business letters, but you should remember that

(a) public authorities are large organizations. This means that reference numbers, cheque numbers, dates and all identification matters are particularly useful to them.

(b) usually your letter will be in answer to theirs. Their letters tend to be complicated and your answer may commit you, eg to the Income Tax authorities.

It is therefore most important to study their letter carefully, to understand what it says and to decide exactly what to answer.

If your answer has to be accompanied by various documents, at the end list what these enclosures are:

Enclosed: 3 passport-size photographs,
          1 birth certificate,
          1 cheque No. . . for £. . . dated. . .

instead of just '5 Enclosures'.

(c) and make sure that you have provided an answer to *all* the questions that are asked. It can be useful to fill in the answers in pencil first; it is so easy to put the answers in the wrong place, (dates for instance), and it is easy to erase a lightly pencilled error without leaving a mark.

4. Writing a job application

This may involve you in filling in a form, in which case treat it in the same manner as an official letter. On the other hand it may be left entirely to you how to write.

Suppose you are applying for a job in answer to an advertisement in the press. Construct your letter in such a way that it helps the selector to get at the key facts. It pays.

Write a covering letter saying where you saw the advertisement and the date on which you saw it; this shows you are systematic.

Give your reasons for applying and, if already employed, why you want to change. State any points which may be in your favour, such as willingness to go abroad, driving experience and outside interests.

Give the names and addresses of at least two people who can be contacted for references. This is very important. Preferably your last employer, or the present one. Your headmaster or your tutor. And one responsible person who has known you for a long time. You must, of course, ask these referees beforehand whether they are prepared to vouch for you.

Enclose a passport size photograph of yourself (with your name written on it).

On a separate sheet with your name, address and telephone number give your curriculum vitae, ie all the relevant factual information about yourself.

1. Give your *age* (you may be too young or too old to be considered).
2. Give your *nationality* (it may be important because of work permits or for other reasons).
3. Give your *marital status* (married applicants may be preferred or excluded).
4. Give your *education* with the name of your school, college, university, the dates you were there in brackets after each. Then give the subjects you studied and your grades. Unversity graduates need not list their 'O' and 'A' levels. However, an 'A' level in, say, French or Statistics, etc should be mentioned if it is an additional qualification to the final degree (eg to have an LLB with an understanding of geology might be an advantage.)
5. Give your *experience:* list the jobs you have done with the dates in brackets. This is how the letter of application with its enclosures should look.

The Managing Director   address

. . . .

. . . .   date

Dear Sir,

In answer to your advertisement in *The Times* of . . . . , I wish to apply for the position of Personnel Manager.

I am 29 years old, British, unmarried.

My reason for applying to you is that I feel the need for change. Bloggs is a small family firm which does not offer enough scope for promotion.

For references please contact my present employer, Mr Bloggs (address), and Mr Smith (address).

Yours faithfully
signed
(JOHN BROWN)

Enclosed: 1 passport photograph and my curriculum vitae.

JOHN BROWN   *CURRICULUM VITAE* (on a separate sheet)

Born 1 March 1950

Manchester Grammar School (1960–67)

A in German 'A' level, B in Spanish 'A' level.

1 year on an estate in France doing farm work, while waiting for University admission.

Fluent in French, German, Spanish.

Manchester University (1968–71)

2/1 in Sociology.

Spent University vacations working as waiter in Germany and Spain.

Secretary Manchester Drama Club.
Swam for the University.

Joined Bloggs and Co as Personnel Officer 1971

Outside interests: foreign travel, driving.

8. Summarizing and taking notes

How to write a summary

To summarize a text is to use as few words as possible to convey its main meaning or the information it contains in the most effective manner.

The *Financial Times* is famous for its front-page, left-hand column; it gives the summary of the world's news so efficiently that no other reading is needed to be kept informed.

Sir Winston Churchill used to expect his staff to 'put everything on one side of a sheet of paper'. This requires great skill besides a thorough understanding of the issues and of their relative importance.

It is not enough to cut out all the irrelevances and the unnecessary words. Indeed, in many cases there are no irrelevances or unnecessary words in what you have to summarize. Therefore it is necessary to condense.

In order to condense one has to re-write, in one's own words, at much shorter length. This means discarding everything of secondary importance in the original text. Once this is done, one must compose, so that the summary reads smoothly instead of being a string of disconnected sentences.

When one is ready to compose, one must not refer back to the original text because of the temptation to use the original words instead of one's own.

There is very little room for quotations in summaries.

The only exception is when the proceedings of a meeting are summarized.

This kind of summary is called Minutes (see chapter 11).

Let us take as an example how one would write a summary of 'Macbeth' in less than 60 words (note that the word Macbeth is put in inverted commas when it stands for the name of the play but not when it stands for the name of the character).

Macbeth is a successful general, tempted by the ambiguous prophecies of witches into treason. Helped and pushed by his wife, he kills the King of Scotland and usurps his throne. He then imposes a reign of terror. His wife goes mad and kills herself. Macbeth is finally killed in fulfilment of the witches' prophecy he had thought impossible. (58 words)

To say it is by Shakespeare, that it is a tragedy, that Macbeth is the hero, or the anti-hero, and that it is well-written, is to comment, not to summarize.

No short summary can give the full meaning of the original. My 58 words do not show the complexity and the richness of Shakespeare.

How to take notes

Notes provide facts for future reference. Note-taking helps to concentrate attention during lectures and, for some people, is of great assistance to learning.

Different people have different reasons for taking notes, and to a considerable extent the reason dictates the way in which the notes should be taken. There is no hard and fast rule. At one extreme there are people who take infinite trouble to make their notes look impressive, so as to make themselves learn by heart; at the other extreme there are people who never look at their notes again. However, for most people the techniques described below should prove helpful.

There is a difference according to whether notes are being taken from:
— a book or journal;
— a school lecture;
— a university lecture;
— a public lecture.

Taking notes from a book or journal

If the book or journal belong to you, mark the passage you need to remember or want to refer to later on. If necessary, write comments in the margin. (Personally, I record at the beginning of the book the numbers of the pages I have marked and sometimes, if the index is inadequate, or missing, the subject of those pages. This saves time later on.)

If the book or the journal does not belong to you, to mark it would be very wrong. Instead, slip bits of paper at the relevant places or jot down on a piece of paper the number of the page and paragraph. It is advisable to read the entire text before copying the relevant passages because this may save unnecessary copying. There may be a more apt passage further on, or what seemed relevant at the beginning may cease to be so in the light of subsequent information.

Incidentally, when taking notes most people invent their own abbrevations. Everyone knows that *wld, shld, thru, govt* or *&* stand for *would, should, through, government* or *and*. Depending on the subject and on how often the same words occur, one can invent handy short-cuts. (I use ♀ for woman, ♂ for man, ♀⃗ for people, M⁰ for moment, CW for Commonwealth, the Greek letter φ for philosophy, = for equal, ≠ for different, // for parallel, /// for similar or same, △ for triangles, ↗ for increase or grow, ↘ for decrease, → for towards, ↗ for against. . .) Moreover, when taking notes there is no point in writing out every word. Leave out everything which is not essential to the meaning. 'The Roman Catholic church still has the power to mobilize great masses of people in two areas of the world: Communist-run Eastern Europe and largely army-run Latin America. One and a half million people turned out to greet the Pope when he arrived in Mexico on January 27th' would thus become in note form: 'RC church still has power mobilize ↗ masses ♀⃗ in 2 areas world: Communist-run E Europe and largely army-run L America. 1½m♀⃗ turned out greet Pope Mexico Jan 27.'

Taking notes from a school lecture

The pace of a school lecture is slow because the teacher wants the students to learn and remember as much as possible. There will be repetitions, examples, and quite often parts of the lecture will be written on the black-board or projected on a screen to make copying easier.

However, to take down everything the teacher says is impossible, unless it is done in short-hand. It is, therefore, very important to listen and try to understand what is being said, so that you only make notes of the important points. Sometimes you only have time to scribble down key words. In such cases you should expand your notes as soon as possible while your memory is still fresh.

There is no need to note what you already know.

Taking notes from a university lecture

There are basic differences between school and university lectures. First of all the university lecturer talks much faster because he expects his audience to take down only the bare facts. Since he assumes more general knowledge, he will be more selective and, unless he enlarges upon a special aspect, he will not give the facts. These can be looked up. Indeed he will usually refer to source material, perhaps even write the title of the book or journal on the blackboard. He is not trying to teach everything there is to know on the subject; instead he is guiding the students. This means you have to concentrate more than at school and be more selective. Usually, besides a few facts or quotations, the lecturer is providing a valuable structure and references which are worth noting.

However, in subjects like chemistry, physics, mathematics, philology or languages, despite increased complexity, the pace and method of university teaching remains very much the same as it was at school and so does taking notes.

Taking notes from a public lecture

The kind of notes taken at a public lecture depends upon the kind of lecture and the reason for attending it. It may, for instance, be useful to jot down a good joke in order to use it yourself when appropriate.

Especially after a meal, taking notes helps concentration and prevents you falling asleep!

In all cases, notes should be taken on loose pages or on index cards. The notes should give the source of the information contained in them with the date, the subject, the name of the book and its author, the page number or the title of the lecture and the name of the institution addressed and the lecturer (when not a regular teacher).

Loose pages should be used instead of bound ones so that they can be arranged, like index cards, according to subsequent needs. It is desirable to write only on one side of the page (as distinct from the card, which ought to be a complete record and therefore may require writing on both sides) because this makes it possible, without destroying information on the other side, to cut out relevant passages and position them where they are wanted.

Some people have a visual memory, some can only remember what they have understood, others remember by association. When the facts to remember are disconnected or have to be learnt in a certain order, mnemonics can be of great use. Mnemonics are tricks to help memory.

This is a trick to help you remember the Kings of Britain since 1066 in order:

> Willie, Willie, Harry, Steve
> Harry, Dick, John, Harry Three,
> One, two, three Neds,*Richard Two,
> Henry 4,5,6, then who?
> Edward 4,5, Dick the Bad
> Henry 7,8, Ned the lad,
> Mary, Bessie, James the Vain,
> Charlie, Charlie, James again,
> William and Mary, Anna Gloria,
> four Georges, William and Victoria,
> Edward and in 1910
> George, and Edward and George again.

(*Ned is short for Edward.)

This is a mnemonic to remember the signs of trigonometric functions:

All Stations to Coventry gives the first letter of each: (*Angle, Sine, Tangent, Cosine.*)

The musical mnemonic sentence *Fat Cats Get Drowned at Ealing Baths* gives the order of sharps in the key signature (F,C,G,D,A,E,B.) And *All Cows East Grass* (A,C,E,G) stands for the four spaces in the base line, just as *Good Boys Deserve Fun Always* (G,B,D,F,A) stands for the five lines in the base line. Well known too, is the verse *Thirty days hath September, April, June and November* which lists the months with 30 days. And to help spelling there is *i before e except after c* (of which *perceive* and *niece* are good examples). Generations of artillery instructors have relied upon *TALAMIEF* to teach gunners to fire (*Target, Ammunition, Line, Angle of sight, Method to choose gun for getting target range, Interval, Elevation, Fire.*) Mnemonics are particularly useful when logic or deduction cannot be relied upon.

Notes to learn

Some people learn by writing, others by looking, other by dint of sheer repetition. For those who learn by writing, copying their notes makes good sense. For those with visual memory, underlining key words in various colours can be useful, as well as making little drawings.

Notes for revision before examination

Such notes should be easy to locate and to follow. Their purpose is not to teach but to remind. Therefore key quotes, dates, equations, formulae should stand out. For example Queen Marie-Antoinette's remark that the poor clamouring for bread should eat cake is worth noting as a reminder that during the French Revolution there was widespread economic hardship because harvests had failed, and the ruling class was cut off from the masses.

Here are notes actually taken at school by a sixth former preparing 'A' level history. The lesson was on *The scramble for Africa from the Afro-centric point of view.*

1. several types scrambles
2. white man's technological progress
   (a) railways (expand)
   (b) steamship (sea, river, Suez canal)
   (c) telegraph
   (d) medical advance (quinine)
3. by-product of (2) was to cut cost of transport by 90% (Tsetse fly made horses impossible) eg Uganda railway to sea allowed shift from gold, ivory and slaves to bulk goods: cotton, cocoa, coffee etc.
4. result of (3) increase in scramble — eg Kitchener survived because Railways, Gordon died.'

These notes taken during class can be expanded later when, for the sake of being complete, facts already known should be added. There is no point noting what you already know at the time; it is better to listen and concentrate on new facts. Moreover, the process of sifting information while taking notes forces you to think. This helps you to learn and to remember in a way just listening without applying your mind does not. For example, short-hand typists who take down every word often have to wait until they have transcribed what they have recorded to know what it was.'

Taking notes for essays, theses or reports

If the subject has been given, taking notes is greatly simplified. For example, if the subject is the importance of Nelson in British naval history, notes from lectures or books should concentrate on Nelson's strategy, naval training, the kind of boats available, etc. His love for Lady Hamilton is not relevant. Therefore, in biographies on Nelson look for relevant data in the index and skip the rest. If, however, the subject you will have to deal with is not known at the time of taking notes, these should cover a much wider field. In all cases when you take notes leave room for subsequent additions. It may seem wasteful, but if you write on one side of the paper only, you will find the blank pages very useful when revising.

Notes for essays are not different from those for theses or reports. The only difference is in content and extent. The more complex the notes the more important it becomes to be able to use information in a flexible way. You should leave room on the page for additional notes. If you use cards, keep them loose in boxes, grouped together by subject or alphabetically. If you use sheets of paper, use punched sheets and keep them in a loose-leaf binder. (A cheaper alternative is to thread wire or a shoelace through the holes.) Loose pages can be moved about (like cards) and new material is easy to insert, neither of which is possible with a bound exercise book.

9. Writing an essay

An essay is the presentation of reasoning.

There are different kinds of essay:

— narrative essays;
— descriptive essays;
— expository essays;
— argumentative essays.

From the point of view of the student the argumentative essay, the essay in which he has to present a thesis, is the most interesting; the one, too, which occurs most frequently in examinations. We shall therefore take that kind of essay first.

A. Structure of all argumentative essays

Always in three parts:

(a) introduction — short;
(b) main part;
(c) conclusion — short.

(a) In the short introduction, present your thesis.
(b) In the body of the essay (main part), present the arguments supporting your thesis.

1. Each argument must be stated at the beginning of the paragraph.
2. Each paragraph must be introduced by the last sentence of the previous paragraph.
3. There must never be more than one thought per sentence, and one idea per paragraph.
4. The arguments must be set out in logical order.
5. Each argument must be illustrated with typical examples. However, do not give more than two or three examples. You are *illustrating* a point, not showing off how much you know. If you want to impress the reader by the extent of your knowledge, this is best done by

choosing examples which are less well-known, or examples which do not come from books, etc but from your personal experience.

(c) The conclusion should be short and confirm, from the evidence in (b), the thesis you set out to prove in (a).

Let us take a fairly straightforward example where the facts are clear so that they largely dictate your answer:

Which factors should a local authority take into account in allocating land as between car parks, for which a charge is made, and recreation grounds, to which admission is free? ('A' level Economics, London, 30 minutes).

Introduction

What is the problem? Is it land use or raising money to plan the *best* use of land? The financial aspect is almost irrelevant to this case. (Money can come from rates, grants. . .) Therefore the local authority should only take the needs of its community into account.

Body of the essay

Let us now look at:

1. The arguments for a car park.
(a) No room to park.
(b) Shops require room for parking.
(c) Get stationary cars off the street.

2. The arguments against a car park.
(a) They attract traffic.
(b) The streets may not cope with greater flow of traffic.
(c) The desire to encourage people to use public transport.
(d) If that land goes to a car park it cannot become a recreation ground (transition to next set of arguments).

3. The arguments for recreation grounds depend on the existing availability of suitable open space. This probably varies according to the kind of local authority.

(a) Village.
(b) Market town.
(c) Big city suburb.
(d) Big inner city area.

Conclusion

In a village without good traffic flow the car park is desirable, it will prevent stationary cars congesting the streets.

In a small market town ditto, especially since this will stop outsiders from parking on the streets, while the car park, by encouraging shoppers, becomes an economic asset to the community.

In big cities lacking suitable open spaces in the centre, where streets are already heavily congested by traffic, there is a strong case against car parks which only attract more traffic. Moreover, recreation grounds are needed for people to relax and children to play. Therefore, as already stated, money is not relevant; the only issue is: what is the best land use under the particular circumstances?

Now let us take a case where the facts are not so clear because we are dealing with human motives, so that various interpretations are possible. In such cases it is very important that you do not just repeat some text book but that you think out which interpretation *you* favour.

The Hindu-Muslim conflict in undivided India was based on class and not on religion. Discuss.
Are you going to say:
A. No
B. Yes
C. Both class and religion

A. The Hindu-Muslim conflict in undivided India was not based on class but on religion

1. Introduction
State your thesis.

2. Body of essay

List the arguments you can think of:

(a) Let us look at the leaders of both sides: Nehru and Jinnah. They were similar types; both Western educated, rich, lawyers, members of the Congress party (Jinnah eventually resigned). (To point out that both were widowers and had an only daughter would be an example of introducing irrelevant facts.) Then how were they different? (Transition)

(b) They were different. Nehru was a Hindu, Jinnah a Muslim. Elaborate what this means in terms of approach to politics. However, both were agnostics, therefore (transition) there must have been another reason than religion.

(c) Both were ambitious (give examples) and only *one* could become Prime Minister. Nevertheless, personal ambition would not have been enough (transition) — they had to mobilize support.

(d) What kind of support did they get? In many respect the same people on both sides.

Jinnah $\begin{cases} \text{educated Muslims} \\ \text{lawyers, landlords} \\ \text{Muslim masses. (give examples)} \end{cases}$

Nehru ditto but Hindus.

Therefore we cannot say there was a class difference in their following. What was it then that their following was based on (transition) which led to conflict?

(e) If it was not based on class it must have been based on a mixture of religion and politics. In the event of free India getting universal adult franchise, the Muslims, who are a minority (quote figures), were afraid of being ruled by the Hindu majority. It was this fear Jinnah exploited (quote speeches) precisely because Nehru's agnosticism (examples of actions and speeches) made him dismiss the importance of religious fears. (example of 1937 Ministry in the UP)

3. Conclusion

Therefore, as can be seen from above, the Hindu-Muslim conflict was not based on class but on religion.

B. The Hindu-Muslim conflict in undivided India was based on class

(This is a Marxist analysis.) Same treatment of the essay in (A), but who were the leaders?

(a) Nehru, a socialist.
(b) Jinnah, a capitalist.

Who were the followers?

(a) The Muslims were less educated in Western terms than the Hindus. Quote Sir Sayed Ahmed Khan and his fears.
(b) The Muslims are a minority (figures). Jinnah's followers were feudal landlords. Nehru's followers were merchants and industrialists as well as Untouchables and landless labourers.

Conclusion

Economic interests were at stake. The Muslims were afraid of economic domination; therefore it was a class conflict.

C. The Hindu-Muslim conflict in undivided India was due both to religion and to class

Introduction

It is difficult to arrive at a clear-cut conclusion because the conflict owed as much to religious as to economic fears.

Body of the essay

1. Let us look first at the religious factors. Extract the relevant arguments from essay (A).
2. However, there was more to it than just religious fears. The Muslims were also afraid of economic domination. Extract the relevant arguments from essay (B).

Conclusion

It can be seen from the above arguments that religion combined with economics to produce conflict. Therefore, it was both a religious and a class conflict.

In the case of essays B and C, remember to have transitions for each new argument as shown in essay A.

Argumentative essays may be written for different purposes. The purpose affects how you write them, although the structure is not affected by the purpose. (Remember: *always* three parts: a *short* introduction, the main arguments in the body of the essay and then a *short* conclusion.)

In the main, essays may be written for one of three reasons:

1. The essay is set in an examination

In that case you are presenting your point of view to readers (examiners) who are familiar with the subject and know more than you do. You do not have to cross every *t* and dot every *i*. If you quote the Oedipus complex you do not have to add that was Freud's idea. But if you quote some obscure research paper you must expand and say who wrote it.

2. The essay is a thesis or a school project

It may still have been set by somebody else, eg the teacher, but you have had time to study the subject and do some research. You can still assume some knowledge in the reader, but you should not assume too much. The facts will be fresher in your mind than in his. If you have yourself chosen the subject, eg in a school project or a university thesis, you may know a great deal more about the details than the reader. The less you think your reader knows, the more you must set out your facts in detail and give your sources. Suppose you quote the changing role of fathers as proof of men's increasing insecurity in the face of women's emancipation and easier divorce, you should state that this idea comes from Professor Mary Douglas and if you can give the title of her book, do so.

3. The essay is addressed to a lay audience, eg an article
   for a newspaper

Assume no knowledge whatsoever, explain all the terms and never
make more than three points. Three points is all an article can take.

Here is an example of how you must assume no knowledge in this kind
of essay: *Mr Nehru, the Prime Minister of India, told the General
Assembly of the United Nations that. . .* is how you have to spell it out
for a lay audience. If you were writing an essay for your teacher/
examiner it would suffice to write *Nehru told the UN General Assembly
that. . .* Your reader knows that Nehru was a man, that he was Prime
Minister of India and that UN stands for United Nations. The reader of
a newspaper article may see the word Nehru for the first time and not
have the foggiest idea of what UN stands for.

As we have already said, argumentative essays can be written for
different purposes, but the purpose does not affect the structure, only
the amount of details you give to the arguments.

Now let us go back to the other kinds of essay.

(a) Narrative essay;
(b) Descriptive essay;
(c) Expository essay.

Each of these requires a different approach, although there is bound to
be some overlap. These three kinds of essays do not call for the
structure in three parts of the argumentative essay because no arguments — or ideas — are discussed.

The easiest of these three is the *expository essay,* provided, of course,
that you know the answers to the questions asked and that you can
express yourself simply and clearly.

Example of how to write an expository essay:

'Explain briefly the meaning of the following:

(a) loss leaders
(b) manufacturer's *direct* sales
(c) after sales service

(d) status equiries' (*'O' level Commerce, London, 30 minutes*).

(a) Loss leaders are goods sold cheap, sometimes at a loss, to attract customers into the premises.
(b) Manufacturer's direct sales are made by the manufacturer to the retailer without intermediaries, ie wholesalers or stockists.
(c) After sales service is the service provided to maintain and/or repair the goods after they are sold.
(d) Status enquiries are enquiries to find out the amount of credit which it is safe for suppliers to extend to customers. For example, in the case of private individuals holding credit cards or cheque books, it is customary for shops to check by telephone before accepting payment above a certain amount for goods taken away at the time of sale.

Note that in each case the answer to the question begins by giving it the same letter as in the original text and that the question is included in the answer, ie '(c) what is after sales service' — '(c) After sales service is. . .' This is of great help to the examiner, who does not have to flip back to see what question '(c)' was.

The *narrative essay* is an essay which tells a story. To tell a story is to record what happened. You may add some information: how it happened, why it happened, but these are details compared with the actual plot and should therefore be kept in proportion. *The sequence of events is the frame-work* of the narrative. It provides the paragraphing and, so long as you follow the sequence of events, you should not have too many problems of composition. The problems you have to settle before you start to write are of two kinds.

(a) selection;
(b) length.

Example: *Your day*. Here is a rough outline:

(i)   getting up (washing, dressing, breakfast);
(ii)   going to school (walk, bus or cycle);
(iii) lessons, break, school meal, lessons;
(iv)   return home, meal, homework;
(v)   evening spent with family or friends, watching TV, playing

games or going for a walk;
(vii) bed.

(a) Select what you think important enough to be mentioned, (the very act of writing implies a selection) and try to make it interesting if you can, eg you had to run for the bus and when you caught it discovered that it was full so that you had to run all the way to school. But if you had no problems getting to school it is only worth a couple of words saying how.

(b) Plan how much time and space to give to the various parts of your essay. You do not want to end the day at, say, lunch because you have run out of time.

Before we turn to the descriptive essay, I want to quote a passage of prose which falls in between narration and description. I am quoting it because it illustrates not only how the sequence of events provides a structure for the narrative essay but also the kind of qualities required to make descriptions vivid. (Arthur Grimble *A Pattern of Islands* John Murray, page 102.)

'Shark'
'There is a four-fathom bank of Tarawa lagoon where the tiger-shark muster in hundreds for a day or two every month. . . You can watch their great striped bodies sliding and swooping with arrogant ease not six feet under your keel. They range in length from nine to fourteen feet, with an occasional giant of seventeen or eighteen feet among them. There is nightmare in the contrast between their hideous size and the slack grace of their movements in the glassy water. Their explosions out of quietude into action are even more atrocious. An evil shape comes gliding below you, smoothly, negligently, as if tranced in idleness; the next instant, one monstrous convulsion has flung it hurtling into attack.

Tigers always do cruise around banks where the smaller fish swarm, but not usually in hundreds. . .

The land in that part of Tarawa is cut by a tidal passage lagoon and ocean. When the springs flood high through the passage, they bring riding in with them from outside a minute marine organism, which settles along the shallows (and) makes tempting food for millions of tiny soft crabs that live on the water's edge. Great hosts of these, none much bigger than a sequin, are lured by the bait an inch or so deeper into the sea than they usually venture.

The next scene belongs to the teeming sardines. Perhaps they too have mustered in their millions because of the tide-borne foods, or perhaps they know that the coming of the food spells crabs in the shallows. Their battalions, massed like silver clouds in the two-foot shoals, charge wave upon wave to the lip of the tide bent upon nothing but the massacre of crabs. But sardines make just the food the mullet love best. The mullet have been massing for their own purposes a little farther out. they plunge in among the sardines, a ravening army of one-pounders. The small fish twist and scatter wildly into open water, the bigger ones after them.

And that is why the vivid, blue-backed trevally have come so close in-shore. Their meat is mullet. They sweep to landward of their quarry and hunt them out to sea, devouring as they go. But alas for their strength and beauty! Engrossed in their chase, they drive straight for the bank where the tiger shark are mustered.'

Note the vivid pictures: crabs not much bigger than sequins; the arrogant ease and the slack grace of the sharks swimming in glassy water. . . Note, too, the economy of words when the effect required is a suggestion of quick action; 'Their meat is mullet'.

And now to the *descriptive essay*. There are three kinds of descriptive essays:

— factual technical description;
— description of people and places;
— imaginative description of emotions, feeling, visual impacts.

Factual technical descriptions

This kind of essay is very easy to write so long as:
1. you are thorough;
2. you remember to mention everything that matters;
3. you decide the relative importance of what you have to mention in the time at your disposal;
4. you remember to adjust the words you use to the level of know-ledge of your reader.

Suppose you have to describe what happens when someone is rushed to casualty after an accident. If you mention that a thermometer has been put in the victim's mouth (instead of saying that his temperature was taken) do not leave it there — have it removed and the temperature read. Unless the reader is totally ignorant do not explain what a thermometer is. However, if you mention an encephalogram, unless your reader knows a little about medicine you had better explain. You can do this in two ways:

(a) 'an encephalogram was taken to check on possible brain damage.'
    or

(b) 'an encephalogram was made. (Encephalographs record brain reactions to electrical impulses.)'

To take a more concrete example, describe a pressure cooker to somebody who has never seen one.

You could begin by describing its use and its advantages over conventional saucepans. Next you could explain what it looks like, the principle on which it works (ie steam cooking under high pressure) and end with instructions for its use. The principle and the instructions are the technical parts of the essay and the parts where accuracy and detailed precision therefore matter most. Technical terms like 'weight indicator' and 'vent pipe' must be explained. It is not enough to say 'place the weight indicator on the vent pipe.' You must describe what they look like (and explain what they do) otherwise there could be an explosion.

Description of people and places

This kind of essay does not require as much precision or attention to detail as technical ones.

If you are describing a place try to create in the reader's mind a *picture* of what it looks like.

If you are describing, let us say, a village square, do not just list the houses around it. Try and make these interesting by picking out arresting details. Perhaps old beams, thatched roofs. Try and give the square character, and life (animals, people, flowers, etc). In choosing what to describe keep in mind the overall effect you want to create. If it is a sad, poor, depressing village square, concentrate on the tumble-down aspect of the houses, the weeds, perhaps a rubbish heap and a cripple or a beggar. To stress the gloom make it rain. Alternatively, use dazzling sunshine to underline the contrast between nature's radiance and the desolation of the site.

If you are describing a person, you must mention the main points which identify that person: sex, size, age group, special features (red hair, wooden leg, large scar on cheek, etc). You must also convey the impact that person makes on first sight. The best way is to give an example of behaviour. 'She enters the room quietly, slinking into a corner hoping nobody will notice her.' Your point that she is shy has been made. By contrast, 'The door swung open as he strode noisily into the room, made a bee-line for the best arm-chair, spread his legs as he sat down, and interrupted our conversation to tell a joke.' That man is obviously unpleasant, a show off, and most insensitive.

Here is an example from *The Leopard*, a novel by Guiseppe di Lampedusa.

> 'She was moving slowly, making her wide white skirt rotate around her, and emanating from her whole person the invincible calm of a woman sure of her own beauty.'

Here is another way of describing a character: by letting it speak. The foolish helplessness of David Copperfield's mother is revealed in the passage already quoted on page 28.

> 'Then, turning affectionately to me, with her cheeks against mine, 'Am I a naughty mama to you, Davy, am I a nasty, cruel, selfish, bad mama? Say I am, my child, say 'yes', dear boy, and Pegotty will love you: and Pegotty's love is a great deal better than mine, Davy. I don't love you at all, do I?'

No sensible, responsible adult talks like that to a child. Moreover, the way she goes on suggests that she is pretty and spoilt. It is most unusual for ugly people to be so self-indulgent.

> 'Leopold Bloom ate with relish the inner organs of beasts and fowls. He liked thick giblet soup, nutty gizzards, a stuffed roast heart, liver slices fried with crust-crumbs, fried hencod's roes.'

James Joyce's character is already defined as a man fond of eating and, from his liking for the kind of food described, it can be deduced by those familiar with orthodox Jews that Bloom must belong to the

Jewish community, though he does not have to be orthodox. Most people retain a liking for the food of their childhood.

There are many ways of describing people. When using physical characteristics, as distinct from behavioural ones, pick those which are relevant to the character.

> '. . . a stout blooming old lady, who looked as if she were well skilled, not only in the art and mystery of manufacturing home-made cordials greatly to other people's satisfaction, but of tasting them occasionally very much to her own.' (*Pickwick Papers*)

Cordials are home-made alcoholic drinks; 'occasionally' is used ironically by Dickens to suggest that she drank quite a lot. One can almost see that fat old woman with her bloated features highly coloured by drink.

Perhaps the most striking example in English literature of a physical feature suggesting character is the use Dickens makes of Uriah Heep's hand.

When David Copperfield first meets him he notices '. . . a long, lean, skeleton hand'. He then sees Uriah Heep closing the office and on parting gives him his hand. 'But oh, what a clammy hand his was! As ghostly to the touch as to the sight! I rubbed mine afterwards, to warm it, *and to rub his off.* It was such an uncomfortable hand, that, when I went to my room, it was still cold and wet upon my memory.' Later on he again refers to 'his damp fishy fingers'.

Heep's slimy hands match his slimy character.

Describe an emotion, a reaction, a sight (falling in love, a sunset)

This kind of essay looks deceptively easy. It does not require knowledge and the structure is what you make it. However, do not fall into the trap. Nothing is more difficult than descriptive creative writing. To succeed, you must produce a picture or a mood, in words. This requires a special gift. Homer spoke of the 'rosy-fingered dawn.' He was a genius. His picture of the dawn has become a cliché; to copy him is out of the question. Forget about pink fingers and reject all clichés in creative descriptions. Indeed, my advice to most of you —

though not to all of you — is to leave creative descriptive writing well alone. Here is why.

Look at this 'O' level (*English for Overseas Students,* London) question:
Fire (at least 450 words)

There is no obvious structure and it is very easy to get lost in words. Besides, what are you going to write about? How you *feel* when you look at fire? What fire reminds *you* of? What fire looks like? This is extremely difficult to write because it needs a poet (in verse or prose) to invent images which will *show* fire to the reader. The only easy way of tackling this exam question is to write about the *uses* of fire, which takes the answer out of creative description.

Let us get back to descriptive creative writing.

> 'When the earth could stand no more and the parched soil cracked; when the air was so dry that one could drink a large pitcher of water in a day without a drop of sweat but only some grains of salt on the brow, the horizon would darken one afternoon, and instead of the hot dusty breeze there came a cool fresh wind with the smell of moist dust. The sky became covered with seething, billowing, white-edged clouds, which approached like an angry army. Peals of thunder and long forks of lightning rent the sky, and large rain drops began to fall, at first slowly and deliberately but soon racing madly down to earth till they were like long needles of glass bursting as they hit the ground.'
> (*Punjabi Century* P. Tandon, p 63)

This description of the onset of the monsoon in the Punjab is well written; with the exception of the second sentence and the beginning of the third the use of words is genuinely original, particularly the comparison between rain drops and glass needles.

Bleak House, one of Dickens' less well-known novels begins with this chilling description.

> 'Implacable November weather. As much mud in the streets, as if the waters had but newly retired from the face of the earth. . . Smoke lowering down from chimney pots, making a soft black drizzle, with flakes of soot in it as big as full-grown snowflakes — gone into mourning, one might imagine, for the death of the sun.'

This picture of the weather, the street, the mood and atmosphere is as depressing as a funeral. Note the 'black snowflakes', the 'black rain', the smoke falling instead of rising. By comparing the geological creation of the earth to the mud in the streets Dickens suggests desolation and the absence of life.

If you write like this, you are a very lucky person. You have the rare gift of originality and you must make the most of it and always choose the questions which allow you to show how well you can write.

Originality is a great asset in answering examinations, as in later life, and examiners are always on the look-out for essays which show originality; they will give the highest marks to those who can combine originality with discipline.

10. Answering examination questions

Candidates who are well informed may easily fail to do themselves justice in examinations, often because of nervousness. Observing a few simple rules of procedure can prevent this.

Study the questions

It pays to spend up to ten minutes on studying the questions.
Read *all* the questions very carefully.
To remind yourself that some are alternatives and that others have more than one part, underline the relevant instructions.
Then read *all* the questions a second time and cross out those you will not answer.
List the remaining questions in order of knowledge.
Before you start to write an answer, read the question once more to make sure you have understood it. It is so easy, with examination fever, to misunderstand a question or to fail to notice important instructions.

Choose the questions you will answer

Look for questions to which you know the answers. It helps if you have already done that during the term. Maybe you have discussed them with friends or just thought about them, so you do not have to organize your thoughts from scratch. And if there is a question to which you know only the bare bones of the answer, but which you are forced to include to make up the number, answer that question last.

Suppose you are out of luck. There are no questions you have tackled before, no questions to which you have studied the answers. DO NOT PANIC. You will usually find at least one question which has been put there specially to help people in your position. It is the kind of question which does not require specialized knowledge and which makes it possible to show that you can think for yourself and express your thoughts clearly. These are qualities examiners value much more than a good memory and the ability to repeat what is in the book.

Here are some examples of the kind of questions I have in mind.

Comedy often aims at provoking more than laughter ('A' level English, Cambridge)

There are two ways in which you can answer:

(a) You can quote a number of comedies and show what the author was trying to achieve in addition to being funny.
(b) If you cannot think of examples of comedies you can argue, at the general level, that comedy exposes human foibles and that when power is arbitrary and direct criticism dangerous, to be funny may be safe because being funny involves exaggerating. Human vanity usually protects the author because the object of the satire (comedy with an ulterior purpose is usually a satire) does not recognize himself so long as he is not directly singled out in the plot.

You can then give instances of what you mean:

1. The foible which the author wants to expose is exaggerated until it becomes ridiculous, ie laughable instead of tragic.
2. The situation is altered so that the roles are transposed and it is the servant, not the king, who is a liar, etc.

Let us look at another question which requires only common sense to answer.

Why is it usually more difficult for a manufacturer or producer to sell his product abroad than at home? Give an example where the opposite applies and say why it is so ('O' level Commerce, London)

Here are some of the obvious reasons.

1. He is not on the spot, has no contacts, may not know the language, the habits, the taste.
2. He has to rely on intermediaries, translators, agents, etc.
3. Payment may be slow. Foreign Exchange regulations are tiresome.
4. Price may be increased because of extra packaging, transport,

insurance, Customs dues.
5. Example of exception. Petrol in Saudi Arabia. Reason: few cars in Saudi Arabia and petrol shortage outside. Remember you have to give only *one* example of the exception.

Another question which requires little text-book knowledge. This time it is an 'A' level Economics question (London)

What are the main factors governing the supply of freshly-cut flowers in retail shops on a given day?

The answer must be — as with everything else in Economics — a function of supply and demand.

Supply in this case depends on: time of year, availability of hot-houses, transport, number of people growing and transporting flowers, strikes, power cuts affecting heating of hot-houses and watering of nurseries.

Demand depends on: price, day of the year (eg Mother's day, All Saints, local custom (in some countries people buy flowers often, in others seldom). . .

Finally here is another question which requires only thought and clarity. This one is an 'A' level Religious Knowledge (London) question.

If Moses had been a committee, the children of Israel would still be in Egypt. Discuss

1. If, as the Bible says, Moses was inspired by God it does not matter whether Moses was a man or a committee. The choice of Moses or a committee was God's, and either way His will would prevail.
2. But, if you believe that the Bible is only the record of a great leader's achievement, the effectiveness of a committee versus a leader becomes relevant.

Say what you think of committees — the pros and the cons — and before you conclude say something about Moses's difficulties in getting his way with his own people and with Pharaoh.

Time spent per question

The way in which you divide your time between questions is very important. In some cases the time is put in brackets after each question. For instance, the question on the supply of flowers had 36 minutes allotted to it and the one on Moses 45.

However, when the time allotted is stated, this does not mean that you should go on writing to the last minute. It is always better to allow time to read over what you have written, so that you can correct mistakes, add missing words, put the finishing touches to punctuation, etc.

When the allotted time has to be spread over a number of questions, how you apportion it becomes very important. If you spend too much time on some questions, you may not be left with enough time for others.

Here are some useful tips:

1. If you have, say, four questions and two and a half hours, this means roughly 30 minutes per question.
2. It is better to choose questions where your knowledge fits comfortably into the time.
3. If you can be *sure* that you will be brilliant in one question by devoting 45 minutes to it *and* that you will get the essence of the answer to another question in fifteen minutes, then it might be a good idea to answer those two. This will still leave you with the required time for the other questions.
4. If you run out of time to finish your last question write down the skeleton of your answer with headings, sub-headings and key facts. This is much better than writing up in full, say, the first third of the answer and stopping short. It will show the examiner what you know and he will mark you accordingly.
5. If you know so much that it will take you one hour to answer (instead of thirty minutes), you will not have time to do justice to the other questions. So do not answer that question unless you are sure that you can discipline yourself to answer it in the time. And to make sure, answer it last.
6. Finally, answer the long and important question first when your

mind is still fresh; leave the shorter general questions till the end. You may be tired or have a headache by then and it would be a pity for it to spoil your main answers.

Answer the question

It is so easy to write something which is not the answer to the question that I have no hesitation in repeating once again:

1. Before you start to work out the answer, read the question very carefully and decide what it means.
2. Do not answer *more* than is required.
3. Make sure you answer *all the parts* of the question.
4. Write the number of the question and the sub-questions *clearly* before each answer.
5. Introduce the essence of the question in the first sentence of your answer, eg 'Comedy often does much more than aim at provoking laughter'.
6. Leave a space between the answers to the questions.
7. Avoid irrelevances, eg whether they have long or short stems, are scented or without smell, has nothing to do with the supply of cut flowers in retail shops on a given day.
8. Answer the question, not something else. For instance:

Give a critical account of your favourite periodical, indicating the reasons why you like it. You should make some reference to the quality of the writing found in it ('S' English, London, 1960)

A lovely question! But were you to take the *Financial Times* as your favourite, do not be surprised if you fail. The *Financial Times* is a daily, not a periodical.

Typical questions in English Literature are like the following:

1. *'Great drama is never merely topical.'* Discuss with reference to two or more plays, or
2. *How far and in what ways have characters approached 'tragic stature' in two plays or the work of one playwright you have studied?*, or
3. *Consider the effective treatment of the conflict between generations in two or more plays.*

These three questions come from the Cambridge examination syllabus for 'A' level set in 1977 on English Literature.

The key to all the answers is given on the front page of the paper and it is very easy to overlook it, once you have opened the paper to look at the questions. The key is that this particular examination deals with English Literature since 1785. To quote characters from Shakespeare is therefore to fail the test.

Equally, to confine your discussion to *one* play is to fail.

Read the questions attentively. Question (1) requires you to deal with *at least* two plays. Question (2) requires you to deal with *two* plays by different authors or the works (ie more than two) of *one* author. To answer question (1) you were not confined to *one* author. Question (3) requires that you deal with *at least* two plays but you cannot use examples from a novel.

When you are comparing, or contrasting, you should try to give the same weight and length to each play, novel or character.

Do not get carried away. Do not spend most of the allotted time on one play, one novel, one author. . . Remember that you are not describing, you are comparing.

Make up your mind how wide the question goes and what its implications are. It is no good going wider than the question and it is fatal not to relate your answer to the question.

I once read a most interesting 'A' level essay, well written, and perceptive. It was such a good essay that I had to read it again and refer back to the question to understand why it had got such a low mark.

The question was *Is Lady Macbeth ambitious?* The essay contained no reference to the way Shakespeare presented Lady Macbeth's character; 'ambition' was not mentioned even once. The theme, brilliantly argued, was that Lady Macbeth was so deeply in love with her husband that she had been moved by what she believed to be his wishes. It then showed how the deterioration of his character was the result of her intervention and ended with the statement that Lady Macbeth's suicide was an expiation intended to absolve her husband from his sins.

It was an admirable essay, but it was never related to the question.

Finally, look at the following two questions (*English for Overseas Students 'O' level*).

1. *What makes a good friend?* (60 minutes) at least 450 words.
2. *My life at work and at home* (60 minutes), about 450 words, not shorter, but not much longer.

What is the difference in the treatment of the answers?

In the case of the first question the answer has to be *at least* 450 words long; it can run to 1000 words or more if you like. What it cannot be is 400 words long. That is the meaning of *at least*.

In the case of the second question, the answer must be *about* 450 words long. 445 words would not be too far out, but 700 words would.

To disregard instructions is to ask for trouble.

Now that you have selected and understood the question and decided how long you will spend on it, you are ready to answer it.

Assume the examiner knows the subject

He is testing *you*, not you *himself*. This means that you can assume a great deal of knowledge and do not have to spell everything out as you might when writing for a more general public.

Suppose you have to mention a speech by Nehru. In a newspaper article which has to be understood by anybody you would have to say: 'Mr Nehru, the Prime Minister of India, told the General Assembly of the United Nations. . .' But in an examination paper it is enough to write 'Nehru told the UN General Assembly. . .' Your examiner knows that Nehru is a man, that he was Prime Minister of India and what UN stands for. If the question has already involved the UN (for instance *Discuss India's role in the United Nations*) you could shorten even further: 'Nehru told the General Assembly. . .' This example was discussed earlier (p. 58).

Structure of the answer

Now is the time to put into practice all the rules we have discussed on how to write.

1. Decide what to say
2. Plan the structure logically
3. Say it simply, neatly, clearly
4. Short sentences with one thought per sentence
5. Paragraphs with one idea per paragraph
6. No jargon
7. If it is an essay, follow the rules in the chapter on essays.

Interplay between generalization and illustration

Begin with the generalization, then give as illustrations the sorts of things which show the kind of evidence upon which your generalization depends.

For example: *What would you identify as the principal obstacles to industrialization in underdeveloped countries?* (*'A' level Sociology, London,*)

One paragraph might be:

'One of the main obstacles to industrialization in the developing countries is the lack of the necessary attitudes. Indian aristocrats despise making money; African peasants do not have the habit of punctuality.'

A complete proof of this generalization would require a book. All that the illustrations do is to tell the examiner the sort of facts you have in mind as evidence. How many illustrations you give depends on how long you have for your answer and on how many generalizations your answer contains. If you have only three quarters of an hour, and this generalization is one of ten, you will probably not have time for more than the two illustrations I have given.

If the question was an essay, you had three hours and this generalization was the main point you wanted to make, you would need many more illustrations.

Remember that if you have a series of generalizations, the number of illustrations should be kept in line with the importance of each generalization. If you have two generalizations of equal importance you must not give two illustrations for one and ten for the other merely because you can think of more examples in the second case.

Main types of exam questions and the right approach to them

The different kinds of essays and how to deal with them have been dealt with in the previous chapter.

Summaries (see page 44)

When you summarize, direct speech must become indirect speech with all the resulting changes in pronouns and tenses.

Example: summarize in about 100 words the following speech:

The Prime Minister, in a party political broadcast for Labour last night, said:

'As you know, during the last few weeks speculation has built up about the possibility of a general election this autumn. Some time ago, in the summer, I said I would make a statement on the future after the summer holidays and this morning I met the Cabinet and conveyed my views to them and now I would like to tell you personally how I see it. First of all, you may wonder why, as this Parliament has a year to run, this speculation started at all. Really it was inevitable as soon as the Liberal Party decided in the summer that they did not want to renew the agreement with the Government. They have resumed their full independence of action in Parliament and it is not for me to criticize that decision. It is obvious that it makes the Government more vulnerable to defeats in the House of Commons than we were. It was this decision, I think, which marked the beginning of the speculation.

Another, different, reason why people have been saying there would be an election is that things have been getting much better during this year. Inflation is at its lowest level in years; there have been tax cuts during the summer, and increases in social benefits will take place this autumn. Living standards generally are improving. Now, I have seen it said often, and only today it was written again, that I have rigged this temporary election boom in order that I shall win. That is false.

The benefit the country is experiencing today is a result of your efforts and the Government has eased the situation because we thought the economy could stand it and for no other reason.

This can be a lasting, not a temporary, improvement if we follow through with consistent policies, so I am not proposing to seek your votes because there is some blue sky overhead today.

Obviously all parties want to win a general election when it comes but let us think for a moment of the great domestic issues the country faces now and ask ourselves whether a general election now would make it any better this winter.

Would a general election now make it easier to prevent inflation going up once more? Would unemployment be any less this winter? Would a general election now solve the problem of how to deal with pay increases during the next few months?

Would it bring a sudden dramatic increase in productivity? No. There are no instant solutions. Advertising slogans are no substitute. The Government must and will continue to carry out policies which are consistent and determined, which do not chop and change, and which have brought about the present recovery in our fortunes.

We can see the way ahead, I spelt it out this week at Brighton; with prices more stable, steadier growth, the increasing advantage brought by North Sea oil, with good foreign exchange reserves, we can foster industrial confidence and we have already laid the foundations to create a better life for all our people.

I know we have large and positive support in the country for the way we are facing these problems. So when I met the Cabinet this morning I invited ministers to prepare themselves for the fifth and final session of this Parliament. It will begin in the autumn. We shall make proposals to carry forward our social policy. We have already made arrangements for increases in social benefits in November. We shall ask Parliament to approve the preparations for holding the referendums we have promised for Scotland and Wales on the setting up of assemblies. We shall work with the greatest vigour to control inflation, reduce unemployment and improve the efficiency and prosperity of British Industry.

We shall face our difficulties as we come to them. I can already see some looming on the horizon. I cannot, and do not, promise we shall succeed. I can say we shall deserve to. Basically, I want to say we go on because we are doing what is best for Britain.

So, I shall not be calling for a general election at this time. Instead I ask every one of you to carry on with the task of consolidating the improvements now taking place in our country's position. Let us see it through together.'

Here is a summary.

'The Prime Minister announced on September 7th there would be no Autumn election despite the fact that the Liberal Party's withdrawal of support in Parliament was making his government vulnerable. He stressed that the very reasons which led people to expect an election now were those for which he decided to wait. He listed those reasons: inflation had reached a new low, the standard of living was rising, the foreign exchange position was good. General elections would not solve the remaining problems: create more employment, increase productivity, curb inflation, settle pay claims. Therefore he would carry on.' (107 words)

No two summaries will be the same, since you select and use your own words. However, if the summary is much shorter than the words allowed, go back to the original. You have forgotten something important. Put in brackets at the end of your summary the number of words used.

Importance of saying what you think, and why, instead of copying from the book

Usually exams are not mere tests of memory but tests of understanding. What the examiner is trying to find out from your answers is whether you have learnt to think about the facts and to interpret them for yourself. Parrot-like knowledge, not accompanied by understanding, is of little value. This is why you will get a much better grade if you work out the answer for yourself, giving your own arguments instead of reproducing some stock answer from your crammer or your text book. Think of the poor examiner who has to correct hundreds of questions: if all gave the same answer he would get so bored!

11. Taking Minutes

Minutes are the record of business done at a meeting. They should be a short summary of the proceedings and contain the exact wording of the resolutions passed. Minutes must show clearly and beyond doubt what was discussed, done and decided so that the record can be preserved and that those responsible for the management of the organization holding the meeting can be identified. The people responsible are the chairman and the members of the committee which is constituted by Directors or elected spokesmen, according to the nature of the organization.

How Minutes are taken varies with the kind of organization and, within the same organization, with the kind of meeting and business considered. Some Minutes have to be very detailed and comply with the rules under which the organization is set up. With public companies or institutions incorporated under the Companies Act, Minutes, like the procedure at meetings, are rigorously defined; however this does not apply to small voluntary organizations which tend to work out their own rules and keep their Minutes as it suits them.

Nevertheless, it is customary, in all cases where Minutes are called for, to have a chairman and on a committee. In large companies as in small voluntary associations it is the secretary who takes the Minutes. (If necessary from a short-hand typist's transcript). If the Minutes are not circulated to the members before the next meeting they are read out to them by the secretary so that objections can be raised and amendments made. The chairman then asks the meeting if he can accept the Minutes as a correct record of the proceedings and 'approves' them (with his signature), after which they are filed in the Minute book* and the chairman proceeds with the agenda — the programme — of the present meeting.

---

*Limited companies have to keep a Minute book by law.

Minutes should always start with the date, time, place and nature of the meeting. The names of the chairman — or his delegate — the members of the committee present (with their function) should be recorded as well as the names of those who excused themselves. Next should come the names — and function — of those, if any, who were 'in attendance', that is who have been invited to attend because they have a special contribution to make. Finally, if the meeting is public the total number present should be recorded.

The subjects discussed at the meeting should be clearly recorded, the same goes for the resolutions (decisions). It may be useful to number the items on the Agenda in such a way that it will be easy to find them later on, perhaps from an index.

It should always be remembered that the Minutes are a record of instructions for action and that, in many cases, no further sanction is required for action to be taken by those responsible.

Let us take first simple Minutes, those of the meeting of the *Kensington Residents' Association*.

The Annual General Meeting was held at: 6 Princes Place
                                       on: March 30th 1979 at 6 p.m.

Present: Mr Smith, Chairman
              Mrs Brown, Hon Treasurer
              Miss Taylor, Hon Secretary

Apology was received from Mrs Stone who is in hospital but asked Mrs Pebble to present the report of accounts on her behalf.
Mr Bills, Auditor, was in attendance by invitation of the Chairman. 64 members of the Association were present.

Agenda:
1. The Chairman took the Minutes of the last meeting as read and signed them.
2. *Finance* Mrs Pebble acting for the Hon Treasurer reported that there was a credit balance of £50 left after expenditure on mail and incidentals and that it would not be necessary to raise the £1 subscription. The report of accounts was approved.

3. *Auditor.* Miss Taylor proposed that Mr Bills be appointed Hon. Auditor. Mr Ramsbottom seconded. The vote was in favour.

4. *Annual report.* The Chairman reviewed the year's success in getting the Borough Council to:

    (a) close the unlicensed betting shop at. . .

    (b) increase the number of residents car parking bays by seven

    (c) refuse permission to lease number 6 Wright Lane to a foreign embassy

    (d) issue warning to the builders working on said premises not to damage the trees.

5. *Election of the executive committee.* Serving members were re-elected unanimously by show of hands and Mr Cramble, proposed by Miss Taylor was seconded by Mrs Bloggs, was elected in place of Mr Winston who has to retire for reasons of health.

6. *Vote of thanks to the committee*

7. The Hon Secretary will circulate the date and agenda for the next meeting as soon as the result of the local elections is known.

Here is another kind of Minutes, more formal because they cover a statutory body: *Snooks and Walker Company Ltd.*

A meeting of Directors was held at 230 Strand, London WC1 on Tuesday September 16th 1979.

Present: Mr Snooks, Chairman
              Mr Small
              Mr Little
              Mr Plug
              The Secretary

In attendance: Mr R. Price Messrs Sales and Stocks
    (part only)   Mr J. Gould Messrs Checker and Stone

1. Minutes of meetings of Sept 1st and 15th, having been previously circulated to the Directors were taken as read, signed as correct and adopted by the Board.

2. *Reports.* The undermentioned reports were submitted to the Board and approved:

(a) Transfer No 462

(b) Finance No 65/10

(c) Sale No 501

(Messrs Price and Gould here attended the meeting)

3. *Smith and Potts Ltd.* With reference to previous minutes (date. . .) about the proposed acquisition of Smith and Potts Ltd the Chairman referred to difficulties over the ownership of their Canadian factory. Mr Price outlined the problems he had encountered in Canada regarding the transfer of the lease. Discussion ensued and it was decided that negotiations should remain in abeyance until Counsel's opinion was received.

4. *Financial report.* Mr Small presented the figures relating to the financial position of the company and all its subsidiaries. Asked by one of the directors, Mr Gould explained why a large sum had been set aside for 'unexpected contingencies'.

5. *Date of next meeting.* Agreed for Nov 3rd at 10 am in the board room.

In *Appendix I* are Minutes adapted from those of a meeting of the council of a university college. These are both very detailed and extremely precise because they have to be correct in law and stand up to challenge. The reason for reproducing them is that they provide a good example of how Minutes of other associations — such as students bodies or trade unions — should be kept, taking into account variations in the statute under which they have to operate.

The Minutes are not only extensive; they are also very carefully broken into sections and sub-sections for easy reference later on. Even more than lecture notes, Minutes have to be easily and quickly produced whenever required. (See *Appendix I*).

As already stressed, there are many ways of taking Minutes and the ways vary according to the type of meeting and its purpose as well as to the need to keep within the law.

Sometimes, even when Minutes are as extensive as those of that college, it may be necessary to append — that is, to attach at the end — more information. It could be a note of dissent because the person who was overruled asked for his contribution to be on record. It could equally well be because the contribution of a particular member was considered so informative that the meeting decided that it should be put on record.

When decisions are put to the vote this can be done by a show of hands. If there is a count and it matters to record who voted for, who abstained and who voted against, it may be simpler to give the names of the shorter lists — eg at a meeting of 27, if five opposed and three abstained record their names, this is shorter than listing the nineteen who voted in favour.

There are cases in which it is important to give the names of all the directors present because, by statute, directors who do not attend often enough have to resign. On the other hand there are cases, with family firms without outsiders, where the statutory annual general meeting is never held (probably because there would be nothing special to discuss). However, to comply with the law in such cases it is merely entered in the Minute book that the annual general meeting was held on . . . at . . . and all the partners sign. (The Minutes do not mention what was discussed or resolved; indeed no such meeting was held, but the legality has been preserved.)

The Minutes of academic meetings are not all as lengthy and precise as those of our college. This again depends on the purpose for which the Minutes are kept, and on the nature of the meeting.

Here are fairly typical Minutes of a post-graduate seminar. The Minutes of academic discussions, seminars or workshops are difficult to take because of frequent interruptions and departures from the agenda. All that may be required is a general and very short summary of the discussion with credit given only to those who made important contributions. After noting the trend of the discussions the rapporteur must record the decisions arrived at, if any, and record the general trend of the proceedings.

Name of seminar, date, place, time, names of chairman, rapporteur, secretary, list of those present with their designation and the university to which they belong.

1. Professor E welcomed the following, A, B, C, D, introduced them to the local members of the seminar working on the project and thanked them for accepting the university's invitation to participate, especially those who had flown in from distant lands.
2. Professor E introduced the subject of the seminar with a short summary of the techniques with which the research group was setting out to evaluate the contribution of rural women to economic development.
3. Discussion followed. There was general agreement that women are overlooked by the planners of developing countries because (a) these are men, (b) village women seldom attend meetings, (c) interviewers are men, (d) male outsiders usually are denied access to village women, (e) the local men they interview take women's work for granted.
4. Professor Z argued for women investigators and women ministers for rural development.
5. There was unanimity on the need to educate rural women. Illiterate women cannot take advantage of existing opportunities.
6. Legal reform is needed.
7. Miss FQ presented a summary of the findings of her field work on women's participation in Bolivian villages.
8. Doctor JS described the work done in Indonesia to introduce functional literacy by combining reading and sewing classes.
9. Date of next seminar was set for Colombo. Invitations to attend would be sent out with full details three months before seminar.
10. Vote of thanks.

12. Using data

'Data' are things known or assumptions made from which it is possible to draw inferences or conclusions. This is why the collection of data is a key point of research.

To be of any use data has to be reliable, relevant and meaningful. Collecting facts for their own sake can be futile. In a book on the Indian village[1], Table IX gives a breakdown by sex of the number of goats aged one year, of those aged one to three years and of those over three years of age. Table X gives the somewhat mystifying information that the village under study had 52 male fowls, 233 female fowls and 105 chickens. Could it be that chickens, like angels, are sexless? Moreover, the author forgot to give a table with the age or sex breakdown of the humans in that village.

Data is best presented in tables or graphs. These should always be numbered for easy reference and should always carry across the top a heading so worded that the information it contains is obvious. The top of each column should also make clear the nature of the information contained in that column.

Example

Wangala wedding expenses for four selected households

Item of Expenditure	Magnate		Middle-farmer (rich)		Middle-farmer (poor)		Poorest	
	Rs	%	Rs	%	Rs	%	Rs	%
Food	874	31	663	32	543	45	97	36
Clothing	367	13	890	42	205	17	61	22
Ornaments	1,139	40	274	13	303	25	68	25
Functionaries	103	3	43	2	5	—	—	—
Miscellaneous	383	13	240	11	162	13	46	17
Total	2,866	100	2,110	100	1,218	100	272	100

(Epstein, T Scarlett (1962) *Economic development and social change in South India* Manchester University Press, p. 103)

[1]Dube, S C (1955) *Indian Village* Cornell University Press

This is a well laid out table; note that when percentages are given, they must *always* add up to 100.

There is no point in repeating in the text *all* the information contained in the table (or graph). But one can make very effective use of selective quotations to emphasize a point. For example, one could highlight the fact that there is a striking difference in the amount spent on ornaments at weddings by a magnate (40%) and a rich farmer (13%) whereas in all four categories surveyed a considerable amount was spent on food.

There is no point in using data to spell out the obvious. For instance, if the census figures show that in a particular village 90% of the children of school-going age attend school there is no need to make a special entry of the 10% who do not attend school. Instead, according to what is being stressed either quote the 90% or the 10% but not both. On the other hand, since data has to be meaningful, if 99.8% of the children do attend school it would be in order to say that *all* children of school-going age go to school because 0.2% is a meaningless figure; perhaps one child had a cold the day the count was taken.

Always remember that statistics must be valid. If in a scientific experiment measurements can only be made with a 5% margin of error, it would be unscientific to quote results in decimals which go beyond the margin of error. What applies to science applies equally to non-scientific data.

Finally, a very useful hint for disposing of data which might be too cumbersome:

Anything which would detract from the flow of the text can be put at the end in an appendix[2], whether it is a table or a text, so long as reference is made at the appropriate place that further information or examples can be found in the appendix. On page 91 I have put in the appendix the Minutes of a college because to have left them in the main text would have upset its balance. If you have more than one appendix give each one a number.

---

[2]Briefer notes may be put at the foot of the page (footnotes) or at the end of a chapter. They may be denoted by a symbol, eg an asterisk * or, if there are more than one or two, by superscript numerals.

13. Making an index

The word 'index' comes from the Latin and means pointer. Usually at the end of books which are going to be used for reference there is an index or an alphabetical list of contents. The purpose of such an index is to help the reader to find quickly the information he requires.

A good index is a very valuable addition to a book. However, a bad index is useless. I remember a government publication which listed 'No onions for Government House' under 'N', as well as 'Three per cent afforestation' under 'T'. Obviously the person who compiled that index had listed the first word of each paragraph instead of trying to understand what indexing is about.

There are three ways in which one should tackle indexing. First, there is the straightforward way of entering, in *alphabetical order,* the literal information contained in the text. To take my above examples of stupid indexing, 'No onions for Government House' has no place in any index, but 'afforestation' does — under 'A'.

Next there is the *cross-indexing* of information. Here is a good example of cross-indexing —

> Armed Forces, see also British Officers, 185, 226, 227, 237, 242, 249, 508, 509; Partition of, 255–65, 309, 330, 333, 503, 507, 511
> Army, Indian, see also Armed Forces, Indian National Army, 139, 176, 180, 202, 208, 226, 227, 232, 233, 242, 245, 296, 321, 333, 397, 416, 449, 507, 508, 533, 534
> British Officers in Armed Services, 226, 255, 256, 262, 333, 409, 416, 457, 508, 510
> Indian National Army, 205, 248–55, 276, 512
> (Hodson, H.V. (1968) — *The Great Divide* Hutchinson)

Note that 255–65 and 248–55 means that the subject is referred to in 255, 256, 257, etc and in pages 248, 249, 250, etc until 255 inclusive.

The above examples are taken from a book on the partition of India. However, to include the word 'India' in the text would be meaningless since the whole book is about India. The same applies to 'Partition' which only appears in the index when it refers to a special aspect of partition such as 'Partition committee' or 'Partition council'.

Thirdly, one should index by *subject*. Even if a word or name does not appear but is in fact covered, those pages should be listed under that word. For example, 'contraception' covers 'Family planning', 'IUD', the 'Pill', 'Vasectomy' etc.

Finding information from the Index, as distinct from the Table of contents, can save a great deal of time. However, if the table of contents is sufficiently detailed, as in this book, our index is unnecessary.

Compiling the index is easy. All you need are the numbered page proofs of the text, two coloured pens or pencils, lots of small pieces of paper (cut into two inch squares) and index cards.

Step one: Equipped with two colours of pencil or pen, read the text carefully and underline in one colour each word or name you intend to put in the index. With the other colour scribble in the margin the subject or subjects covered in that page.

Step two: Copy on to your small pieces of paper, the underlined words and the page numbers, one word to a piece of paper. If the same word appears more than once on the same page you need not copy it again. With the other coloured ink or pencil write the subject and its page on a separate square of paper.

Step three: Sort out the pieces of paper alphabetically. You will have to include the subjects as well as the actual words or names you underlined.

Step four: Make an index card for each word or name and enter on it the pages on which that word appears in numerical order, as well as the subjects in alphabetical order and their page numbers in numerical order.

> *Example*
> Attlee, C. R. (Earl Attlee):
> Appointment of Lord Mountbatten, 189–201, 302; Viceroy's Instructions, 545–7; other references, 87, 94, 129, 133, 176, 186, 305, 309, 314, 329, 335, 357, 461, 468, 515
> (Hodson, H. V. *The Great Divide*)

14. Making a glossary

A glossary is an alphabetical list of technical and foreign words with their explanation. If a glossary is called for, use a third colour when marking the text and underline the words you want to explain. There is no need, when copying them on to pieces of paper, to enter page numbers, but keep to the third colour to distinguish them from the index. Arrange in alphabetical order and give the explanation after each word.

Allah   Islamic expression for God.
Arya Samaj   Modern reformist Hindu sect based on the Vedas.
              Founder Dayanand Saraswati.
Ashramas   Four stages in the life of a Hindu: celibate student
              stage, householder stage, hermit stage, beggar stage.
Atma   Soul or spirit.
Brahmacharya Period of celibate student education. First stage in the
              life cycle of a Hindu.

15. Compiling a bibliography

A bibliography — the list of the books and articles which have been of help in writing — is always welcome at the end of your text. Including it shows that you have taken trouble to search for information; it also has the advantage of suggesting further reading on the same or related subjects. Serious books usually end with a bibliography which can be put before or after the index.

To compile a bibliography all you have to do is to enter on an index card each book or article you read during the course of your work. Record the surname of the author, with initials (there are many authors with the same surnames), the title of the book, the name of the publisher, the year of publication and, if you can, the date of the latest edition.

To compile the bibliography, separate the articles from the books. You have, of course, recorded the name, number and date of the journal in which the article appeared.

Then arrange the cards in alphabetical order, preferably according to the surname of the author. First, list the books, then list the articles or theses.

The following shows the books I have myself used, listed under the headings suggested above. In the Bibliography of this book, the same information is set out in a slightly different way.

Title	Author	Publisher	Year of publication	Latest edition
First year at the university	B. Truscot	Faber & Faber	1946	1964 — paperback
Scientists must write	R. Barrass	Associated Book Publishers Ltd	1978	2nd edn — 1978
Effective technical writing and speaking	B. Turner	Business Books Ltd	1974	
How to take Minutes	H Graham Helwig	Pitman Publishing Ltd		8th edn — 1975
Written English today	A Leslie	Macmillan & Co	1972	13th edn — 1978
Better English	G H Vallins	Pan Books	1953	4th edn — 1978
Mind the stop	G V Carey	Penguin	1939 (CUP) 1971 Penguin	
The complete plain words	Sir Ernest Gowers	Pelican	1962	2nd edn — 1973
Roget's Thesaurus		Longmans		revised — 1962
Modern English usage	F G Fowler	Clarendon Press OUP		revised — 1965
Concise Oxford dictionary		OUP	1911	6th edn — 1976
'O' Level English Vols 1 and 2	J E Burgess	Leonard Hill	1967	
The presentation of technical information	R O Kapp	Constable	1973	

Appendix 1: Minutes of a university college

The following are Minutes adapted from those of a meeting of the council of a university college. These are both very detailed and extremely precise because they have to be correct in law and stand up to challenge. The reason for reproducing them is that they provide a good example of how Minutes of other associations — such as student bodies or trade unions — should be kept, taking into account variations in the statute under which they have to operate.

The Minutes quoted below are not only extensive; they are also very carefully broken into sections and sub-sections for easy reference later on. Even more than with lecture notes, it has to be possible to find a Minute easily and quickly when required.

Blankshire College
(University of Ipchester)

There was a meeting of COUNCIL in the Council Room on Thursday 15th February 1979 at 16.45.

PRESENT: Sir Cyril Smith, Chairman of Council in the Chair; Dame Jane Read, Vice Chairman; Mr M. Hall, Hon Treasurer; the Principal: Dame Anne Pyms*; Mr J. Bailey; Dame Margaret Pott**; Mrs C. Best; Dr L. E. Benson; Miss A. F. Brown; Mr J. S. Stapleton**; Dr N. J. Slowman; Professor A. B. Jones; Professor N. E. McIntyre; Mr J. T. Moss; Mr S. G. Peters; Mr C. F. Roberts**; Professor M. T. Smith; Professor S. P. Williamson**; the Secretary.
(*from item 3(d); **to end of item 8(c))
In attendance: the Accountant

APOLOGIES for absence were received from Mr M. Kaine Professor Cookson, Mrs B. Pye, Mr A. J. Tympson, Dame Annabel Trott, the Registrar.

ANNOUNCEMENTS:
COUNCIL noted with pleasure:
the award of the OBE to Mr J Jones, a Governor of the College.
COUNCIL learnt with regret:
the death on 14th December 1978 of Mrs W Roussel, BSc, Governor of
the College since 1956. Council asked the Chairman to write to Mr
Roussel.

Agenda Part 1

1. The MINUTES of the meeting of December 14th 1978 were con-
    firmed and signed as a correct record after the addition of Mr J S
    Stapleton's name to the list of those who were present.

2. MATTERS ARISING from the Minutes — Major Maintenance
    Contract (Item 6 of Minutes). A further report from the Contrac-
    tor was in preparation.

3. COUNCIL AND CONSTITUTIONAL BUSINESS
    (a) *Policy Committee — Distribution of Functions*
    On the recommendation of Policy Committee (C/7/79 para-
    graph 1) COUNCIL RESOLVED that Policy Committee
    should remain in being at least until the preliminary Estimates
    of Income and Expenditure, 1979/80, have been dealt with
    and that
    these Estimates be considered at a joint meeting of Policy
    Committee and Finance Committee on 10th May 1979.
    COUNCIL NOTED from C/10/79 Paragraph 2 that Academic
    Board had agreed that its request for increased academic
    representation on Finance Committee could be met by an
    increase in the minimum number of Staff Councillors appoin-
    ted to the Committee.

    COUNCIL would expect to receive at its next meeting pro-
    posals for the distribution of Policy Committee's functions
    among other Council Committees and for appropriate revisions
    to the By-Laws to accommodate these and the increased
    academic representation on Finance Committee with the
    object of formally disestablishing Policy Committee at the

end of the 1978/79 session.

(b) *Participation in College Committees*

Paper C/13/79 T laid on the table reported that it had been difficult to find volunteers to serve on the Steering Committee established by Council at the December meeting (Minutes 5(d)) and suggested that the Secretary's Office should deal with the drawing up, circulation and assessment, of the questionnaire designed to discover what 'the entire personnel of the College thinks about general proposition of participation. . .'

In view of the great importance of the issue Council advised that the Secretary should:
(i) take advice from experts within and without the College on the construction of the questionnaire and
(ii) if further attempts to recruit a Steering Committee proved unsuccessful, obtain Council's approval for the questionnaire before issuing it.

(c) *Rules for the exercise of Jurisdiction over students* C/2/79

On the recommendation of the Staff Student Joint Committee RESOLVED that the maximum fine which may be imposed by the Principal for breach of College Regulations (Paragraph 2 Section B of the Rules for the Exercise of Jurisdiction) be increased from £25 to £75.

(d) *Membership of Council*

Council received with pleasure the announcement that Dame Margaret Pott had been reappointed as University representative on Council for three years from 28th February 1979.

4. UNIVERSITY BUSINESS

University of Ipchester — New Regulations C/3/79

On the recommendation of Academic Board (C/3/79) RESOLVED that the Senate of the University be informed that the governing body of the College consents to the revisions proposed in the report 'New Regulations — Part I'.

5.   RESOLUTION FROM THE COLLEGE UNION SOCIETY
C/4/79
The Personnel Secretary attended for this item. As requested
paper C/4/79 set out the Secretary's comments on the issues concerning the position of non-teaching staff within the College raised
in the Resolution received at the December meeting C/62/78 T
(Minutes item 10) from the College Union Society.

The Secretary further reported that the problems of recruitment
to the Maintenance Staff and the salary levels compared to salaries
paid by other University Institutions (which were not yet covered
by University or intra University Agreements) were about to be
reviewed by Estate Management Committee, through its General
Services Committee.

After discussion during which the Student Councillors asked that
their objection be recorded to statements made in Section 2 Paragraph 1 and Section 6 Paragraph 2 of C/4/79,
the Principal made it clear that in spite of the economy measures
during 1978/79 no established posts had been frozen and that filling
of vacancies in the Maintenance Staff Establishment had only
been subject to the shortage of suitable applicants and the delays
arising from pressure of work on the Personnel Section. Attention
was drawn to the difficulties experienced elsewhere in the filling of
maintenance posts.

COUNCIL RESOLVED that the issues raised by the College
Union Society in relation to the wages and position of non-
academic staff within the College be referred to the established
mechanisms for dealing with such problems ie to the joint negotiating committees, to Estate Management Committee and its sub-
committees and to the Steering Committee on Participation, as
appropriate.

6.   STAFFING MATTERS
COUNCIL NOTED that it had again been necessary to arrange
a special meeting of the Council/ASTMS Joint Negotiating Committee to consider grievances arising from the annual grading
review procedure

and that
there had been a 'Failure to agree' on two appeals against grading
which had been before this Committee.

7. REPORTS FROM STANDING COMMITTEES
    (a) *Joint Policy Committee/Finance Committee C/7/79*
        (The report from Policy Committee alone was dealt with
        under item 3(a))

        (i) *Funding of Departments*
             NOTED adjustments which had been agreed to the present
             system of departmental funding and
             RESOLVED that as a new item of expenditure a research
             contingency fund be established in the sum of £2,500 in
             the first instance (subject to increase by agreement with
             the Hon Treasurer) to support the employment of promi-
             sing research workers for short periods between complet-
             ing work under one grant while awaiting support of a
             second grant or a more permanent post within a depart-
             ment which is firmly expected to materialize within a
             period of three to four months.

        (ii) *Financial Planning*
             NOTED that recurrent grant provisionally announced for
             the three years up to 1980/81 represented very little im-
             provement on the 1978/79 position.

        (iii) *Estimates of Income and Expenditure 1978/79*
              On the understanding that experience in 1977/78 indicated
              that a deficit of this size expected at this stage was likely
              to lead to a near balance at the end of the year RESOLVED
              that the Revised Estimates of Expenditure be approved
              as set out in PC/6/78 RD modified by PC/F/3b/79 R ex-
              pecting a deficit of £93,653 subject to a continuation of the
              careful control of staffing vacancies agreed in October
              1978.

    (b) *Report from Finance Committee C/8/79*
        The Hon Treasurer introduced the Report —
        RESOLVED

(i) that the College Union Society Subscription Fee for 1979/ 80 be at the rate of £28 for full-time and at £14 for part-time students — ie a basic fee of £26 plus improvement element for 1979/80 only of £2

(ii) that the action of the Chairman of Council be confirmed in authorizing *Consultants Fees* of up to £5,000 for the preparation of a report on urgent maintenance work requirements and for preliminary design work on the most urgently needed repairs and improvements.
RECEIVED
The remainder of the Report concerning annual contributions to Student Freshers' Week costs; Appeal; Grants and Gifts; the views of the Standing Committee on Laboratory Expenditure on the appointment of College Safety and Radiation Protection Officers; Technician Salaries.

(c) *Report from Safety Committee C/9/79*
Appointment of College Safety/Radiation Protection Officer
RESOLVED that alternative methods of recruiting to these appointments be pursued, ie that applications received in response to the advertisement for a full-time post authorized by Council on the recommendation of Safety Committee be considered in the light of the response to the internal trawl for two part-time holders of separate responsibilities and that the appointment committee be authorized to choose between the two possible ways of filling the post, taking particular account of the qualifications of applicants for the full-time post and the availability of members of the existing staff to fill the two part-time posts.

8. REPORT FROM ACADEMIC BOARD C/10/79
    (i) *Recognition of Teachers in Medical Sociology C/10/79*
    Paragraph 1
    COUNCIL NOTED the recommendation of the Academic Board and RESOLVED that the six persons named in Paragraph 1 of C/10/79 should be granted the status and title of Visiting Lecturers of the College.

(ii) *Student Numbers at 31st December 1978* C/10/79 Paragraph 9
COUNCIL NOTED that the Academic Board has begun
consideration of a proposed admissions policy which will
enable the College to reduce student numbers by 1981/82 to
the level of its given targets.

A full report will be made to the next meeting of Council on
2nd March 1979.

9. APPOINTMENT OF FELLOWS TO THE COLLEGE
COUNCIL NOTED that under the provisions of By-Law 42,
invitations have now been extended to Governors, Academic
Staff and Senior Administrative and Library Staff to submit nomi-
nations for Fellows of the College for consideration by the Fellows
Sub-Committee.

10. OTHER URGENT BUSINESS
None.

Appendix 2: A test of appreciation

Read carefully the following article dealing with economic growth which appeared in *The Economist* of February 3rd, 1978, and which I believe to be a model of how to write. What features qualify it for such an evaluation?

Going for growth

The first in this new series of schools briefs on the world economy deals with economic growth. After 25 years' spectacular growth, the stagflationary 1970s have posed unexpected difficulties. The less developed countries, where two thirds of the world's population lives, have made some progress, but the rich-poor gap is still unhealthily wide.

One, two, three for growth

Rich countries have got richer at different speeds and times, but the underlying pattern has been the same.

Steady expansion of demand for goods and services (the aim of fiscal and monetary policy, if not always the result) has induced increases in their supply;

Resources, especially labour, have shifted from the primary sector (farming) to the secondary (industry) to the tertiary (services);

Productivity growth was fastest in industry, especially in manufacturing, so that countries which maintained or increased industry's relative importance usually achieved the best overall growth.

But it is now rare to find an industrial country with more than 35% of its labour force in industry, while services account for a growing proportion of both output and employment.

For any country, there is naturally some point beyond which agriculture's contribution to gdp[1] will not fall: if only for security reasons, countries like to grow as much of their own food as possible. But this floor is very low indeed: In America, Belgium and West Germany for example, agricultural output is now only 3% of gdp. At the other extreme, it is over 60% in Nepal and Burundi.

98

Throughout the world, the shift from agriculture has been going on (see chart). Sometimes this is for good reasons — improved agricultural productivity, better opportunities elsewhere; but in some ldcs (less developed countries) it has been also caused by agricultural failure, so that people drift off the land to become unemployed in the towns and cities.

In one important respect, ldcs have not been following in the footsteps of the industrial world. A high proportion of their gdp already comes from the tertiary sector, where transport, utilities (eg, electrical and water) and public administration are large employers. In most ldcs, future economic growth will for a time reduce the relative importance of the services sector (as well as agriculture's). In some cases, that is already happening: in the (middle-income) Philippines, for example, services' share of gdp fell from 46% (1960) to 37% (1976). A few developing countries have even passed through that stage, and the teritary sector is again on the up: eg, Brazil, where it has risen from 49% of gdp in 1960 to 53% in 1976.

Though ldcs' progress along the development route has meant faster growth in the 'middle income' countries than in the already developed world (see first chart), catching-up is a long job. It is made more difficult by higher birth rates in the ldcs. Even on the (certainly wrong) assumption that industrial countries stop growing altogether, it would take middle-income countries, growing at their 1970–76 average, 65 years to match the industrial countries' gnp[2] per capita. For the low-income group it would take 746 years. Assuming, more reasonably, that all three groups grow at their 1970-76 average rates, it will be AD 2220 before the middle-income countries match the industrialized ones: low-income countries would simply slip farther and farther behind.

What does growth mean?

Comparing gnps is not always a true guide to how rich each country is. For a start, some contributions to gnp are peculiar to certain countries. All the energy used to keep people in cold countries warm increases their gnp: in others, nobody has to pay the sun to do the same job.

Gnp comparisons have to be made in a common currency — nearly always the dollar. But exchange rates can fluctuate so sharply that in the short run they may exaggerate gnp changes. Over a longer period they are less distorting — but even so, they only reflect price differences in internationally traded goods and services. The prices of many others — like housing, education and medicine — have an important effect on real incomes. If these are cheaper (relative to traded goods' prices) in country A than in country B, the real (internal) purchasing power of a unit of its currency will be understated by its exchange rate against country B's currency.

If these differences are taken into account, 'purchasing power parities' (ppps) can be used instead of exchange rates to compare gnp figures.

The distribution of 'real' gross world product (gwp) becomes less unequal (see table). The richest 10% of the world's countries produced 45.3% of gwp based on nominal exchange rates, 33.6% on ppps. Although still tiny, the poor countries' share of gwp rose proportionately the most when ppps were used: from 2.64% to 6.97% for the poorest 30%.

For many 'social indicators', like life expectancy and literacy, the moral seems pretty clear: growth is good for you. However, some critics argue that economic and social welfare are not always the same thing — that richer countries show a higher incidence of, eg, mental illness. Others say that this occurs in poorer countries as well: but nobody calls it that, or collects figures about it.

Slowing down

Until 1973, it seemed as though the developed countries had found the key to sustained growth, a key which others could also use. But the bubble was burst by:

Inflation. The quadrupling of Opec's oil prices at the end of 1973 was the last twist to an inflationary spiral that had been gathering pace for two years. In the industrial world, the inflation rate went from 4½% in 1972 to 13½% in 1975; ldcs were similarly affected.

Trade imbalances. Both industrial and developing countries went heavily ($33 billion and $24 billion) into deficit on their 1974 current account, while Opec had a $62 billion surplus.

These two factors meant:

Deficient demand. Opec's surplus carved about 2% out of gross world product, and in the short term proved unspendable. Governments of industrial countries took fright and deflated, ldcs cut where they could and borrowed the rest.

Growth inevitably suffered. In the industrial countries it had averaged 5% a year for 10 pre-Opec years: only 3¾% a year since then. Unemployment has risen, productivity fallen, and investment grown so slowly that many now fear that the capital stock is inadequate to meet a rapid upturn in demand. For all but a handful of nics[3] (and the oil producers themselves), growth in the developing world has also slowed down considerably.

Speeding up

But the world economy is coming back to an even keel. Despite a planned 14.5% rise in the oil price in 1979, the Opec surplus will be not much more than $10 billion. Inflation in the industrial countries has come down to about 6½%. The OECD projects that growth will accelerate this year in the majority of industrial countries (though the co-incidence of a slowdown in the two biggest is bad news for the rest of the world). The chances of the world economy regaining its ability to grow fast and smoothly will be a major theme running through the rest of these briefs.

Away from the farm
Distribution of gdp* at current prices

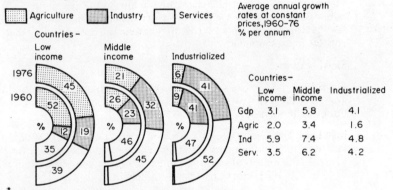

Average annual growth rates at constant prices, 1960–76 % per annum

Countries –	Low income	Middle income	Industrialized
Gdp	3.1	5.8	4.1
Agric	2.0	3.4	1.6
Ind	5.9	7.4	4.8
Serv	3.5	6.2	4.2

*Median volume so figures do not necessarily add to 100%

---

[1] gross domestic product
[2] gross national product
[3] non-industrialized countries

Bibliography

Barrass, R (1978) *Scientists must write* Associated Book Publishers.

Burgess, J E (1967) *'O' level English, Vols 1 and 2* Leonard Hill.

Carey, G V (1971) *Mind the stop* Penguin 4th edn 1978.

Concise Oxford Dictionary Oxford University Press 6th edn 1976.

Fowler, F G (1965) *Modern English usage* Oxford University Press rev edn.

Gowers, Sir Ernest (1962) *The complete plain words* Pelican 2nd edn 1973.

Helwig, H Graham (1975) *How to take Minutes* Pitman 8th edn.

Kapp, R O (1973) *The presentation of technical information* Constable.

Leslie, A (1972) *Written English today* Macmillan.

Roget's Thesaurus Longmans rev edn 1962.

Truscot, B (1946) *First year at the university* Faber & Faber paperback edn 1964.

Turner, B (1974) *Effective technical writing and speaking* Business Books 2nd edn 1978.

Vallins, G H (1953) *Better English* Pan Books 13th edn 1978.

Acknowledgements

For permission to reprint copyright material the following acknowledgments are made:

Going for Growth and other extracts, The Economist
Paid Servant by E. R. Braithwaite, The Bodley Head
Punjabi Century by P. Tandon, Chatto & Windus and The University of California Press
The Great Divide by H. V. Hodson, Hutchinson Publishing Group
A Pattern of Islands by Arthur Grimble, John Murray (Publishers) Ltd.
Economic Development and Social Change in South India, Professor T. Scarlett Epstein

Every effort has been made to trace and acknowledge ownership of copyright. The publishers will be glad to make suitable arrangements with any copyright holders whom it has not been possible to contact.